PARENTING
FOR
PEACE AND JUSTICE

PARENTING
FOR
PEACE AND JUSTICE

James McGinnis

Kathleen McGinnis

ORBIS BOOKS
Maryknoll, New York 10545

Seventh Printing, December 1985

The Catholic Foreign Mission Society (Maryknoll) recruits and trains people for overseas missionary service. Through Orbis Books Maryknoll aims to foster the international dialogue that is essential to mission. The books published, however, reflect the opinions of their authors and are not meant to represent the official position of the society.

Manuscript editor: Robert R. Barr

Library of Congress Cataloging in Publication Data
McGinnis, James.
   Parenting for peace and justice.

   Bibliography: p.
   1. Parenting—United States. 2. Christian ethics.
3. Family—United States—Religious life.
4. Christian life. I. McGinnis, Kathleen. II. Title.
HQ755.8.M43   649'.1   81-3917
ISBN 0-88344-376-7 (pbk.)   AACR2

CONTENTS

ACKNOWLEDGEMENTS

This book is truly a cooperative venture. We interviewed, in person and by questionnaire, a number of parents who have also been trying to link family life with the larger community and world around us. Thanks for their time, thoughtfulness, friendship, witness—to Jerry and Marti King, Ruth and Leroy Zimmerman, Jim and Peggy Herning, Roni Branding, Betty Lee, Josephine Lockhart, Beulah Caldwell, Al Chappelle, Eldora Spiegelberg, Mike and Barbara Richter, John and Sylvia Wright, Elise Boulding, Irene and Bob Tomonto, Antonio and Maud Sandoval, Pat and Jerry Mische, Winnie and Wally Honeywell, Bob and Janet Aldridge in a special way, Dorothy Armbruster, Dave Thomas, Barbara and Gene Stanford, Allen and Joan Deeter, Roy Wolff, Carolyn Shadle for some resources, and Rev. Alphonso Cayetano for help in some of the interviewing.

Special thanks to Tommy, David, and Theresa, who were the inspiration behind this book and the joy behind many of the events described here. It is they who are helping us learn how to accept, love, forgive.

PARENTING

for

PEACE AND JUSTICE

INTRODUCTION

The social mission or ministry of Christian parents was beautifully summarized in the Second Vatican Council's *Declaration on Christian Education*. According to the Council Fathers, the role of parents as educators

> is so decisive that scarcely anything can compensate for their failure in it. For it devolves on parents to create a family atmosphere so animated with love and reverence for God and people that a well-rounded personal and social development will be fostered among the children. Hence, the family is the first school of those social virtues which every society needs. . . .
> It is through the family that children are gradually introduced into civic partnership with their fellow human beings, and into the People of God. Let parents, then, clearly recognize how vital a truly Christian family is for the life and development of God's own people.[1]

But in the total Christian perspective, what this "civic partnership" and this "development of God's own people" are all about is the transformation of the world and the building of the Kingdom of God! Not we, you say, we're too busy! Then how do we read Matthew 25 and the Beatitudes? . . . "Blessed are the peacemakers, . . . blessed are they who hunger and thirst for justice. . . ." Are the Beatitudes too, then, just for people who aren't too busy? Was Jesus addressing only non-parents?

And what will our response be to the statement in the 1971 Synod of Bishops' document *Justice in the World:* "Action on behalf of justice and participation in the transformation of the world fully appear to us as a *constitutive dimension of the preaching of the Gospel*"? Is it for us as parents merely to thank God that there *are* people—other people—who have time to act for justice and transform the world, while we parents handle some smaller thing called "family ministry"?

No, not if acting for justice and transforming the world is a constitutive dimension of the preaching of the Gospel. For there is no Christian who is not called to preach the Gospel.

So Jesus is speaking these words to all of us, parents and non-parents alike. And the church is addressing all of us, parents and non-parents alike. As the parents of three adopted children, ages nine, seven, and five, we have long wrestled with the challenge of integrating social and family ministry. We want to be able to act for justice without sacrificing our children, and to build family community without isolating ourselves from the world. In our nine

1

years of effort we feel we have made some progress in spite of some very real obstacles. This book is our attempt to share with you our effort, our progress—and yes, the obstacles.

Time is the most obvious obstacle. Even for us as a two-parent family with adequate income, time for both social and family ministries is hard to come by. For single-parent and economically poor families, we know it is much more difficult still. When all or most of one's energies have to be spent on economic survival, little is left for much ministering to the other oppressed! This is why we have attempted to include in our book as many things as possible that can be done in the ordinary course of parenting, especially in talking with our children, pointing things out to them, and generally raising their social consciousness.

Closely related to time is the *social context* of family living today. The social and economic structures of our society provide little support for parents, especially economically poor ones. To cite but two examples, day care and mental health systems are underfunded. Schools and police often have such low expectations of the urban poor that violence is actually condoned. As one parent put it:

> Parents must also teach their children methods of survival and strategies for change in a society filled with injustice and exploitation. Parents need to articulate a consistent set of humanistic values and then struggle to live by them *and* teach them to their children. We face the challenge of teaching our children cooperation in a society that pits one racial group, class or sex against another; of nurturing trust in a society riddled with fear; and of promoting assertiveness at a time when apathy and conformity are rewarded. Exploitative child-oriented advertising requires that parents help their children learn what's good for both their bodies and their psyches.[2]

Few parenting books acknowledge this social context. They see child-raising as an individual problem requiring individual solutions and ignore the structural or social level of reality.

A third obstacle to integrating social ministry and family ministry is *isolation*. High mobility combines with an individualistic ethic (nuclear families, with each family on its own) to make real community difficult. Without the support and challenge that community can provide, few people, especially beleaguered parents, are about to go forth to transform the world. Further, often our homes and neighborhoods become castles and ghettos to protect us, as it were, from the world and social problems. When we are "protected" from the victims of injustice and from those who are working for change, the problems seem less real, less urgent.

Closely related to isolation is *lack of imagination*. Many people do not know what to do even when they are willing to do something. "Action on behalf of justice" and "peacemaking" are simply equated, for many people, with either marching in demonstrations or contributing to hunger-relief efforts; and most people are afraid of or disagree with the former and are already doing the latter! "So what can we do?" they ask. The more out of touch we are with the victims of injustice and with people working for change, the less imaginative and less courageous we are likely to be.

This book suggests ways of overcoming some of these obstacles. Regarding time, we hope to share with you many of the ways we have discovered for including our children in our action for justice in ways to which the children can relate. Rather than competing with each other, our social ministry and family ministry enrich each other. That is, the more we go into the world as a family to help build our neighborhood or our world community, the more we are building our family community. And vice versa, we are coming to see that part of our social ministry as a family is to build our family community. Integrating the "apostolic life," the "family life," and the so-called "spiritual life" keeps us from the schizophrenia that sunders the experience of the wholeness of Christian living—the "full Gospel," as some put it.

Where lack of imagination and inspiration are concerned, we hope the examples for action we recount—from our own life and those of other families—will unlock possibilities for others. The multiplicity of suggestions is not meant to overwhelm people by implying that they all should be done. All of us seem to move best one step at a time and, in any case, quality, not quantity, is our concern, as we shall state many times. The multiplicity is merely meant to open the imagination to see a range of possibilities, so that persons or families can decide what integrates best in their situation at this time. Parenting for peace and justice is a long process, not something to be accomplished in a single year.

At this point it should be clear that this book is neither a scientific study nor a child guidance book. It is a personal account of our own efforts at integrating our social ministry and our family ministry. It incorporates the fruit of our years as teachers and peace educators of both children and adults. Finally, it involves the experiences and insights of a dozen other families who also have been trying to integrate social ministry and family ministry.

These dozen families were chosen primarily to diversify the experiences and suggestions we could share. Not all parents are white, middle-class, Catholic, involved in a two-parent situation, heterosexual, with three children all in elementary school, and so on. But we are. So we have attempted to broaden the experiential base of our book by integrating the experience of others.

A point needs to be made about the term "parenting." This term could imply that the responsibility for children belongs with parents only. This is of course by no means the case. We are aware of the important role of other adults (grandparents, other relatives, and others in the community).

Who are we, and how did we come to what we have written here?

We both come from all-white, Catholic, middle-class backgrounds—Jim in suburban San Francisco and Kathy in south Saint Louis. We were both blessed with wonderful parents. We were married in 1967 in our mid-20s while we were both teaching and doing graduate work. We were living in Memphis in 1968 when Martin Luther King was killed; Jim was in the Tennessee National Guard at the time and this was one of many reasons why that killing touched us both so deeply. The Vietnam War, having a cousin among the "Catonsville Nine" draft-file burners, and the Kent State killings were other major events in the formation of our social conscience and consciousness.

At the same time as our social conscience was being formed, we were beginning our family. Thus we were experiencing the call to a more radical response to social sin simultaneously with the call to parenthood. In 1970, the year we started the Institute for Peace and Justice, we also adopted Tommy. David was adopted in 1973 while Jim was doing his dissertation on Gandhi and shortly after our summer in India. Theresa's arrival in 1975 coincided with our decision to move into a fully integrated neighborhood and to send our children to the integrated public school system in University City, a suburb of Saint Louis. Theresa's Black and Native American heritage called and continues to call us to move more deeply into her worlds.

1975 was also the year the Institute left Saint Louis University and became an independent non-profit organization. This was a real year of faith—faith in God's providential love and in the community of people who were helping to support our work as educators, lecturers, consultants, writers, and occasional "activists." It would not have been easy to be suddenly "on our own." Each year since then has been a growth—in faith, in the awareness of supportive friends, in the importance of prayer, in a willingness to act on what we say and write, and in the attention we give to our family community.

There have been no dramatic conversion moments in our lives—just many tiny miracles, steps, and urgings. We fail as often as we succeed—whatever those words mean. We have learned to say no, to be more patient, and to move one step at a time. This book is a sharing of many of these steps.

Each chapter in the book is a dimension of our integration of social ministry and family ministry. The chapters on violence—living nonviolently as a family and dealing with violence in our society—relate more to the peace dimension of parenting for peace and justice. The chapters on materialism ("simplicity/stewardship"), on racism ("multiculturalizing family life"), on sexism ("sex-role stereotyping"), and on social action are concerned more with "justice." The final chapter on prayer is our attempt to integrate the "spiritual life" and the "apostolic life."

In a sense, talking about some chapters as being "more about peace" and others as being "more about justice" creates a false dichotomy. We see the two together, and often call to mind Pope Paul VI: "If you want peace, work for justice." Peace without justice is a negative peace, a false harmony, with the violence of injustice just waiting to erupt. Positive peace (the harmony, cooperation, or unity of different individuals, groups, or nations) is built on justice. By justice we mean the progressive realization of peoples' economic rights (the material necessities of life), cultural rights (their dignity as individuals and as a people or culture), and political rights (their participation in decisions that affect their lives, their being "artisans of their own destiny"). By justice we also mean the progressive realization of people's duty of solidarity—working with others for the common achievement of these rights.

This is who we are and what we believe. The implications of these beliefs for our family life are spelled out in the rest of the book. We hope you will find them helpful and challenging, as we have.

CHAPTER 1

STEWARDSHIP/SIMPLICITY

Terri was six years old. Her cousins came from the East coast for Christmas and gifts were exchanged. But Terri felt something was missing. She went to her room, looked through her "things," and made a decision. Her cousins were excited and somewhat surprised to receive an extra present. The presents were Terri's "treasures"—her swimming ribbons, shells from her collection, and some of her very special rocks.

Rationale for Practice of Stewardship/Simplicity

Basic concepts

This kind of story could be told over and over. There are countless times when children seem to grasp the meaning of stewardship better than adults. Children are often able to transcend the limits of possessions and see the things they have as gifts to be used for others and shared with others. An old verse reads:

> You, little child,
> with your shining eyes and dimpled cheeks,
> you can lead us along the pathway
> to the more abundant life.

That "more abundant life" clearly involves the concept of stewardship: what is mine is not mine for my exclusive use, but for the welfare of others. That applies to our individual possessions as well as to the earth and its resources.

There are two elements of stewardship that are integral to its functioning in our lives. One is the *source* of what we have. The other is our own *accountability* for the use we make of what we have—accountability for our role as stewards.

The writers of both the Old and New Testaments leave little doubt about the source of what we have, about who owns the earth. "The earth is the Lord's and the fullness thereof" (Ps. 24). In Leviticus 25:23 Yahweh speaks very directly: "The land belongs to me, and to me you are only strangers and guests." The message is clear: we do not really own anything. We are *stewards* of the earth and of its rich variety of resources.

As stewards, what is our responsibility? What are we charged to do with the goods of the earth? Saint Paul answered, "What is expected of stewards is that each one should be found worthy of the trust" (1 Cor. 4:2). And how do we measure that worthiness? How do we hold ourselves accountable? In 1854, Chief Seattle of the Suquamish nation addressed this question in a stirring way:

> Teach your children what we have taught our children, that the earth is our mother. Whatever befalls the earth, befalls the children of the earth. If we spit upon the ground, we spit upon ourselves. This we know. The earth does not belong to us; we belong to the earth. . . .
>
> One thing we know, which the white man may one day discover—our God is the same God. You may think now that you own Him as you wish to own our land; but you cannot. He is the God of *all* people, and His compassion is equal for all. This earth is precious to God, and to harm the earth is to heap contempt on its Creator. . . .
>
> So love it as we have loved it. Care for it as we have cared for it. And with all your strength, with all your mind, with all your heart, preserve it for your children, and love . . . as God loves us all.[1]

Chief Seattle recognized not only the connection between the earth and the Creator, but also the steward's responsibility for preserving it for future generations.

Linked closely with the concept and practice of stewardship is that of simplicity of lifestyle, or simple living. Jesus has challenged us to live as the lilies of the field. We are not to spend our time thinking about how to acquire more material possessions. He has also said some direct things about how wealth may get in the way of entering the Kingdom of God. It is more difficult for the wealthy to enter the Kingdom than for a camel to pass through the eye of a needle.

A 1979 statement of the Presbyterian church puts the challenge of Jesus in a modern context.

> We believe Christ calls us to dissent from our present lifestyles and to make a radical break from the patterns of over-indulgence, consumerism and reckless waste. We are called individually and ecclesiastically to choose a lifestyle which more nearly reflects the simplicity of Jesus' life and allows us to identify with the poor and powerless throughout the earth. Such an altered lifestyle enables us to reconsider what we truly value in life, how we measure success, where we live, what we eat, how we use energy, how we invest our lives and resources, and where and how we travel. In short, we are challenged to live more simply that all may simply live.[2]

The interrelatedness of stewardship and simplicity is clear. The dictums of a simple lifestyle direct us to rethink *all possessions*. The challenge of stewardship points us toward using what we have in a different way—for the good of others.

Motivation

As followers of Jesus. The whole of Jesus' mission is a direct challenge to us to live more simply and to be more responsible and accountable for what we have. Certainly the model of the life of Jesus is clear. He was poor. He lived in a poor community. And his life calls us constantly to reexamine what we think we need to have. His words leave little doubt as to what he invites his followers to do. He exhorts us to put our faith in God, not in things:

> So do not worry; do not say, "What are we to eat? What are we to drink? How are we to be clothed?" It is the pagans who set their hearts on all these things. Your heavenly Father knows you need them all. Set your hearts on His Kingdom first, and on his righteousness, and all these other things will be given you as well [Matt. 6:31–33].

In his parable about the rich man who spent his time building bigger barns so he could accumulate and hoard more things, Jesus warns, "But God said to him, 'Fool! This very night the demand will be made for your soul; and this hoard of yours, whose will it be then?'" (Luke 12:20). And certainly the parable of the talents directs us to examine what we are doing with the goods of the earth that are our responsibility (Luke 19).

We are also called to reexamine simplicity in our lives because of our role in the redemption of humankind. Gustavo Gutiérrez in *A Theology of Liberation* speaks of the redemptive character of voluntary poverty—the way poverty helps create a oneness with the human family, especially those members who are suffering. It is not that Gutiérrez sees poverty as ideal, or even as good; on the contrary, he is reminding us to work *against* poverty. Nor is he suggesting that those of us who are not poor "play at" being poor. Rather, he challenges us to let go of the privileges we have *at the expense of* the poor. Poverty, he says,

> has a redemptive value. If the ultimate cause of human exploitation and alienation is selfishness, the deepest reason for voluntary poverty is love of neighbor. . . . It is not a question of idealizing poverty, but rather of taking it on as it is—an evil—to protest against it and to struggle to abolish it. As Ricoeur says, you cannot really be with the poor unless you are struggling against poverty. Because of this solidarity— which must manifest itself in specific action, a style of life, a break with one's social class—one can also help the poor and exploited to become aware of their exploitation and seek liberation from it. Christian poverty, an expression of love, is solidarity *with the poor* and is a protest

against poverty. . . . It is a poverty which means taking on the sinful condition of people to liberate them from sin and all its consequences.[3]

Gutiérrez's call to a "break with one's social class" is a strong challenge, one that demands prayerful reflection. What does it mean for us? Are we ready to take some steps? Where can we get support?

As members of the human family. Mahatma Gandhi, the fighter for justice in India and a true champion of the cause of the poor, believed that no one is entitled to own anything that everyone else cannot also own. While that may seem like a radical notion, it certainly does make us take stock of our own standard of living in comparison with that of the majority of the world's people. We in the United States constitute 6 percent of the world's population but consume 40 percent of the world's resources. If we are serious about the earth belonging to the Lord, then we need to look at our obligations in that light. The dictates of justice are clear. We need to find ways to bring about a more equitable sharing of the earth's resources to enable people not only to survive but to thrive. This requires a greater sense of *interdependence.* In our small, immediate families, all the members have to function in an interdependent way; the world community needs this too. We must be committed not only to furthering relief programs for the poor of the world, but also to changing the larger economic and political structures that keep certain people poor. Chapter 6 will treat this concept of structural change, or "works of justice," in more detail. Chapter 3 will talk more about developing a sense of global interdependence within our families.

Goals and Outcomes

Now, the question is how to take these somewhat theoretical notions and apply them in a family context. What specifically may we hope to accomplish with our children in terms of living out stewardship and simplicity? We might propose the following eight goals.

1. Greater concern for life

The more we realize that God is the source of all we have as well as the source of the earth itself, the more profound will be our respect for all living things. It would be hard to take our role as stewards of the earth seriously without seeing the tremendous responsibility this entails for protecting human life. In a family, even very young children can see when people are more prized than things, when possessions are ways to help people, or when too many possessions get in the way of people. This concern for life can also direct us to work to change social and economic conditions that threaten life. *Taking Charge* is a manual for action put together originally in 1974 by a group called the Simple Living Project, an outgrowth of the American Friends Service Committee in San Francisco. In that manual the question of the connection between simple living and working for "life causes" is put in this way:

> Simple living means that our lives can be richer in many ways without being destructive either to the planet or to other human beings. . . . Through freeing ourselves of "thing-addiction" we become less "thing-like" in our own relationships. We also free our energies to contribute in other ways to help end the gross economic inequalities at home and abroad.[4]

One step in this direction might be letter-writing about issues like food stamps or capital punishment.

2. Relationships with others

Just as a simpler lifestyle can foster a greater overall concern for life, so it can free our time and attention for enriching our relationships with others. "Good times" can now revolve around other people rather than around expensive entertainment. The needs of others can take precedence over "this is mine to use for myself." One of the ways we have tried to put this into a fun context with our own children is in our Valentine's Day celebrations. We have given them "I Love You tickets," which name things we will do together—a bike ride, jogging, a trip to the library, cooking a meal, and so on. Thus the emphasis is on the *relation* among us.

3. Self-reliance

The more we are dependent upon possessions and money for our comfort, entertainment, happiness, and security, the less we can rely on our own insights and abilities. The vast potential to be tapped in each human being often lies dormant. We would all say very readily that we want our children to develop to their maximum potential. Yet it seems that often, without intending it, we encumber them with too many *things*. A down-to-earth activity like making a family budget is a way of concretizing a sense of taking charge of an element of our lives—how we spend our money. Making a budget can also be a way of acting out a sense of stewardship: good stewards are accountable for what has been given to them. Keeping a careful accounting of precisely where money goes is a struggle (efficient record-keeping not being a strong point for either of us), but we are working on it. And we see a need to involve the children in it. Other parents have told us that they have successfully involved their children in budget discussions, and that their children's attitude toward money and the spending of it changed significantly as the children became more aware of how much things cost and where the money went. They became more responsible about their own spending.

4. Personal growth and self-awareness

One of the long-range and continuous outcomes of a simpler lifestyle is an opportunity to be more aware of ourselves, our motivations, and our every-day patterns, conscious or unconscious. This requires time—time to think, to pray, to read—time to get in touch with our inner selves. This time is the gradual outgrowth of depending less on *things* to fill our days, and gaining more and more control over our lives. We think this is an especially important consideration for women. Many women, especially mothers, go through their days being very attentive to the needs of others but giving very little attention to their own needs, especially to their need for time alone to think and pray. That is symptomatic of a society and a culture that has cast women into the position of always thinking of their own needs as secondary.

An exercise to help us as adults become more aware of how we fill each day is suggested in *Taking Charge.*[5] It is called a "time log," and it is a written record of what we do during a day in one-hour intervals. Then we are to look at what we have recorded and answer these questions:

1. What five activities took the most time?
2. What did I enjoy the most?
3. What would I like to be doing more often?
4. How much time did I give to meditation/prayer?
5. What activity would I like to be doing but I am not?

This exercise might be one to do with older children, or to discuss when finished with older children.

5. Development of community

A crucial element in any attempt at family stewardship and simplicity is the development of community. In a society like ours, the only effective way to be able to cut down on possessions, to view what possessions we do have in a different way, to give ourselves a basic level of security while creating desir-able alternatives for ourselves and our children, is to work at it within a sustaining and supporting community. Building community on a personal or neighborhood or parish level is also a way of concretizing the concept of interdependence—how we need each other. In a sense, the development of community becomes both a goal and a means to a goal.

There are different kinds or levels of community. No one can say which kind is best for anyone else. That discernment must be done by each person and each family. Three kinds of community are as follows:

Living community: This is a living arrangement wherein a number of peo-ple actually live together under one roof. This kind of community is ob-viously a very close-knit group, where not only household tasks, often in-cluding child-care, but even income, are divided among all the members. We ourselves have never been part of a living community. Friends of ours who live in this kind of community stress its strengths in terms of reinforcing the shared values of simplicity, social action, and prayer life, and the breaking down of sex-role stereotypes (who can best do what job). But there are also struggles involved in building this kind of community. The more people that are involved in the community, the greater is the number of personal relations that need attention, cultivation, time. The necessity for continued open communication among all members of the community is paramount.

Physical proximity: In this kind of community people live near enough to one another for some real sharing and concrete mutual support—some meals together, common prayer, shared child-care, shared transportation, and the like. It is a "neighborhood" in the traditional sense, where people really care for one another.

Community of spirit or concern: This kind of community building is probably the most understandable and the most workable for the majority of people, especially in a beginning stage. It involves some kind of identifiable signs that a group of people are together in spirit and are supporting one another. Friends of ours here in Saint Louis have such a community. The adults from a number of families gather once a week for prayer. The children are involved through fun activities like a camping trip or a softball game. Both adults and children have also been involved in the preparation for one of the families' adoption of a child from India—from praying for a safe arrival to chipping in to defray the expense. Also, adults and children have worked together to provide a simpler Christmas celebration for their families.

Our own family's attempts at community building have been small steps in one sense—but important ones for us. At various times we have belonged to prayer communities with other families, and an integral part of that was common celebrations of all adults and children—Thanksgiving, Christmas, a Seder supper at Easter. Currently we celebrate a children's liturgy with three other families once a month. We also get together with the parents in this group once a month to discuss parenting. Another small step we have taken or tried to take is that of our "food co-op." A *real* food co-op is a big organizational endeavor. Our attempts have been more modest: we buy cheese in quantity once a month, along with about a dozen other families in our neighborhood. A babysitting or child-care co-op in which child-care responsibilities are traded off is another small step that friends of ours have made in community building.

The example of a prayer community has been cited several times, but deserves more explicit attention here. There are different kinds of prayer communities, but the basic theme is one of people coming together in prayer to share their faith, their joys, their struggles. It is often through a prayer community that people have challenged and supported one another in a variety of lifestyle changes and social-justice actions.

6. Creativity

The encouragement of creative impulses and activities is a major concern for many parents. How does this relate to stewardship and simplicity? We have found (and friends of ours who have worked at this for a much longer time and more systematically have found) that the more we as parents strive to deemphasize the importance of possessions in our lives, the more we are forced to find substitutes or alternatives. We are put in touch with our own inner resources. Dorothy, a friend of ours, says she feels her efforts in this regard have had a lasting effect on her children. All of her nine children, from six to twenty-eight, have a genuine respect for their own creative abilities. She feels they all have developed a sensitivity to the beauty around them as well as a confidence about what they can do with their own hands.

Some critics of our possession-oriented culture refer to our attachment to things as a form of addiction. There is certainly much truth in that, since, as with any form of addiction, other elements of one's life are blocked out or neglected. We are very likely to leave undeveloped our appreciation for beauty, our sense of artistic expression. *Taking Charge* states it well: "Creative simplicity involves developing our own tastes, rather than letting them be formed by advertising and other social pressures which stunt imagination and discourage self-expression. Simple living is a re-discovery of our creative and imaginative energies."[6]

7. Energy conservation

Another outcome of a concern for stewardship and simplifying our lives is conserving energy. We have noticed in our children a growing awareness of the ways in which we use energy (car, heat, lights, cooking, and so on), along with an insistence that we be more careful about them. Our nine-year-old, for instance, is vigilant about turning off lights. (We realize there is a big element of power in that vigilance, probably outweighing a concern for stewardship!) We have also found ourselves just recently beginning to talk to the children about mass transportation—what it is, why it helps the overall energy situation, etc. We feel strongly that the more children are involved in discussion of energy matters, the more they will be able to see small things they can do to make a change.

8. Better health

Many of the health problems that adults and children face in our society are related directly or indirectly to over-consumption, and to simply not being good stewards of the gift of our own bodies. Weight control clinics and clubs, groups that support people who want to stop drinking or smoking, medical programs geared to repair damage we have done to our heart and other parts of our body, are all testimony to the fact that our health would be a lot better if we changed our habits of consumption. We shall address the question of diet a little later in this chapter. Meanwhile, one other practical health concern is the question of medicines. Have we fallen into a pattern of over-dependence on drugs like aspirin, cold medicine, cough medicines, or ointments? One simple exercise is to check the contents of the medicine cabinet. Is everything there necessary for someone in the family? Or again, have we become overly dependent on a doctor's advice? Do we model and encourage for our children healthful and simple activities and recreations— jogging, biking, walking, other sports?

Other Strategies

The hardest question for many of us when we talk about simplifying our lives is "How?" Specifically, what parts of our lives are we talking about? And how do we go about taking a first step, or taking more steps once we have gotten started? In this part of our chapter we would like to suggest some "how" answers in a variety of areas. The questionnaire with which we begin is intended to raise issues; there are no "correct" answers. It is the process of asking ourselves the questions that is important.

1. What skills do I have that I would like to share with others?

2. When was the last time I shared something I knew how to do with someone else?

3. When was the last time I learned a new skill?

4. If my children could have anything they wanted, what would they want for Christmas? Where do their desires come from?

5. How many things do I (we) own which are worth over $200 (average annual income of the poorest third of the world's population)?

6. Outside of school, what are the three activities which involve most of my children's time? Are these activities active or passive?

7. If I were to classify my possessions in two categories—*(a)* those which promote self-reliance and creativity and *(b)* those which promote passivity and more consumption—which category would be the largest?

8. What are my five favorite forms of recreation? Which of these costs over $2.00 each time I do it?

9. How much time each day do I spend watching TV? How much time each day do my children spend watching TV?

10. How many clothes do I have that I have not worn in the past year?

(Some of these questions were adapted from *Taking Charge.*[7])

Questions like these (and there could be many more) can direct us in looking at our present patterns and deciding whether or not there are things we would like to change.

The following suggestions are directed toward specific things we can do and/or support others in doing.

1. Diet

Simplicity about food is a complex matter. Frances Moore Lappé in *Diet for a Small Planet* says:

> A change in diet is a way of experiencing more of the *real* world, instead of living in the illusory world created by our current economic system, where our food resources are actively reduced and where food is treated as just another commodity. . . . A change in diet is a way of saying simply: I have a choice.[8]

Our own experiments with food have met with varying degrees of success. We have tried to involve the children in the planning of the meals. Each week each person in the family plans one meal. We try to emphasize a balanced meal, so a little nutrition education comes into the planning. We also stipulate that if the meal a person plans was a meat meal last week, then this week it must be a meatless one. We see this as a way for the children to have real decisions to make, as well as a way of encouraging them to see a variety of foods that are "good to eat." It is also a way of introducing them to some of our own reasons for wanting to cut down on meat consumption. Lastly, it helps cut down on meal-time grumbling.

We also decide each week on an after-school-snack menu. The children select the daily snacks and we post a list on the refrigerator. The only sugar items that are allowed are graham crackers and the ice cream in a milkshake. This system has helped put a dent (but we emphasize, only a dent) in the sugar and junk-food addiction that is so much a part of children's lives. A sample week's list might read:

Mon.: Peanut Butter Baggugos (A marvelous concoction of ½ cup peanut butter, 2 tbsp. honey, ½ cup raisins, and 2½ tbsp. dry milk, rolled in coconut or sunflower seeds and chilled in the shape of a log in the refrigerator.)

Tues.: Popcorn

Wed.: Fruit of your choice

Thurs.: Milkshake

Fri.: Peanut butter and graham crackers

We have a vegetable garden every year (sometimes successful, sometimes not). Gardening is a very tangible way of acting out stewardship, of creating a greater awareness of the abundance of the earth, of putting us more in touch with the earth, and of stirring more interest in vegetables for children. (Our youngsters are much more excited about eating vegetables from our garden or Grandpa's garden than those purchased at the store.)

We have participated in many vegetarian pot-luck dinners. (Our children are pot-luck lovers.) The variety at these dinners is encouraging and exciting for adults and children alike.

2. Clothes

Consider this quotation about clothes from *Taking Charge:*

> The American public spends $60 billion a year on clothes, enough it would seem to drape the earth, yet for all that money American clothes are often uncomfortable, unuseful, unhealthy, and don't express our unique personalities. . . .
> It is convenient to buy new clothes at a local store, but it is costly, in many ways. Aside from the money involved, you pay the price of turning your back on your own creativity. When you buy clothes off a rack, you leave your personal expression undeveloped. Some clothing industries are notorious for exploiting workers, which also puts a price on the clothes you wear. In order to avoid paying union wages, many manufacturers send their work to foreign countries to take advantage of the more easily exploited unorganized workers.[9]

What can we do?

Many families take full advantage of second-hand clothing stores. Besides supporting a way of recycling clothes and cutting down on expense, second-hand stores often support needy organizations. Hand-me-down or second-hand clothes often provide opportunity for creativity through patching or redoing in some way.

We are fortunate in having a Grandma who makes some of our clothes, as well as friends and neighbors who recycle clothes through us, and we try to do likewise with our own outgrown clothes. Somehow the idea of using and reusing clothes is a community builder. We have spoken with friends who are able to do the same thing effectively with teenagers—even with the tremendous clothes pressure that is part of adolescence. One couple, Wally and Winnie, said this about their twenty-year-old son Mark: "He discovered Goodwill one day when we sent him with clothing for the poor. He now looks first at Goodwill for clothing, and has taken his brothers with him. He also challenges *us* to buy our clothes at Goodwill or not buy at all!"

3. Availability of what we have for others' use

The parents of Terri, whose story begins this chapter, have built a beautiful one-room cabin in the country about seventy miles from the city. Their attitude toward the cabin is that besides their own family of eleven using it, it must be available for others to use. So teachers from the city bring groups of students out to be surrounded by natural beauty, and other individuals and groups use it for meetings and retreats. To us, their example is a striking one of stewardship.

A system of pooling tools or books or records, so that these items can circulate, is another way of increasing the availability of "our" things. Parishes or congregations can set up such a pool. Our parish is beginning a pool of services in which parishioners sign up for the services they are willing to provide for others in the parish—transportation, grocery shopping, laundry, mending, and so on. Other kinds of talents could surely be included in a "Parish Skills Bank"—electrical work, baking, knitting, plumbing, carpentry, auto repair, and the like. This is an opportunity for community building, as well as a way to say that stewardship involves the use of our talents as well as our goods.

4. Recreation

We have tried (with mixed success) to interest our children in those toys, games, and outdoor activities that maximize creativity, activity, the development of physical capabilities, and encouragement of the team concept—and that are inexpensive. In doing that we find ourselves often using public facilities like parks and libraries. We are trying to say to our children that they do not need to own things in order to enjoy them. Caring for library books and records, or playground equipment, not because they own them but because others use them too, is a simple yet profound *experience* of stewardship for a child.

We say "with mixed success" because we have succumbed to some pleas for what we would call "flashy" toys, to some trips to the movies, and so on. But we have been trying to encourage family game time, one or two evenings a week, as a better way to have fun.

One more idea—connected to the family-game-time concept but going beyond it—came from *Family Adventures Toward Shalom,* by Discipleship Resources. There we read about "family repair night"—an evening a month for the family to work together repairing things—toys and/or household items.[10] We see it as a way of having fun while working together, maybe topped off with popcorn and hot chocolate.

5. Money

Earlier in this chapter we discussed the concept of budgeting as an example of stewardship. Our friends Wally and Winnie have told us about a simple budgeting technique they and their four teen-aged sons use. After they first decide they want to buy something, they wait a week to see if they still want it—a curb to impulse buying. We try to let our children in on some of our criteria for spending money: "This toy will help you think of other things to do"; or "This used bike still has a lot of riding left in it and it only costs about half as much"; or "We don't want to spend money on this doll because the way it's dressed makes you think it's very important to have new clothes."

6. Home

Those of us who are fortunate enough to have a home may well feel the imperatives of stewardship and simplicity as applying to this "possession" too. Simplicity demands we look at the way we furnish and decorate our home. Children can help build furniture or track down second-hand pieces. Older children can and should be included in discussions about decorating, remodeling, or buying a new appliance.

But the ultimate question in the concept of stewardship of our home is how to make it available to others to use. The answers are as varied as people's lifestyles and family situations. We know people who have taken in foster babies; had teenagers living with them for short periods of time; offered a home to a pregnant woman who had no other place to go; made it a practice to seek out people who were lonely and invite them to share a meal; have an "open home" with regard to neighborhood children or school friends of their own older children. All of these are examples of having "Christ Rooms" in our homes—havens for people who need a place to stay.

7. Nature

Chief Luther Standing Bear of the Oglala Sioux said years ago, "Lack of respect for growing, living things soon led to lack of respect for humans too."[11] Conversely, encouraging children to respect and enjoy the earth and all the beauties of nature is a way of encouraging stewardship and a respect for all life.

Finding more ways to enjoy ourselves outdoors in all seasons is becoming more and more important to our family. A Winnebago Indian mother suggested to us several years ago that we spend *quiet* time with our children outside, not "doing" anything, not even walking, just *being there,* and listening and thinking. We have just begun to try to do this with the children, especially with one child at a time. Other nature-related activities—hiking (especially early morning walks when everything is so fresh and new), time in a park, camping, developing interests in trees, flowers, rocks, animals, and so on—are relatively simple things, yet they really help us and our children touch the beauties of nature in a different way.

8. Energy use

Our children have participated in our recycling efforts since they were very young. (Many of our friends make better use of their bikes for errands, taking their children along, than we do. That is one of those "things in the future" for us.) We turn our thermostat down in the winter, try to hold off using our window-unit air conditioner as long as we can, and sometimes remember to tell the children what we are doing and why. Two good sources for more energy-saver ideas are *99 Ways to a Simple Lifestyle,* Center for Science in the Public Interest, 1757 S Street, N.W., Washington, DC 20009 (1976), pages 1–68, and *Taking Charge,* pages 36–43.

9. Celebration times

We have found the *Alternative Celebrations Catalogue* to be an inspired resource in the whole area of creating celebrative times with our children that are more centered on people and self-giving than on things. Gift-giving times, whether birthdays, Christmas, Hannukah, weddings, or the like, are good opportunities for expressing creativity and individuality. One family we know with older children give each other clothing for gifts, and give only to extended family and friends, at Christmas. At other times they give gifts of "love-letters," in which they tell someone how much he or she means to them. We have many friends who make the most of their gifts in ways like these. We try to do it as much as we can ourselves and encourage the children to do the same. We were so thrilled when Tommy drew a picture and composed a poem for Jim for his birthday last year.

Birthdays are especially meaningful times for children. We have another "mixed success" story with our attempts to decommercialize birthday celebrations. When Tommy was six we gave him the choice of inviting a few friends to a party-with-presents or inviting a lot of friends but without presents. Not only did he choose the latter, but he decided to make presents himself for each guest. But it was a different story the next year. When we suggested that he was too old at seven for a lot of presents from his friends he strongly presented the opposing view. In the preceding month he had been to three parties where his friends had all received a lot of presents. It was just too much for him to go without what all his friends received. So we agreed that his seventh birthday could be a party-with-presents. And he agreed that the presents could be things made by his friends, or used toys.

At Christmas we try to focus on Christ and de-emphasize the "Give me" aspect of Santa Claus. Our children have all believed in Santa Claus, but he has become Jesus' delivery person. Our special family trip during the Christmas season has been to view a light display at Our Lady of the Snows Shrine across the river in Illinois. The display includes a crib scene and a children's Christmas movie about Christ's birth. Families we know have settled on a variety of ways to celebrate Christmas. We think the important elements in them all are:

—Christmas is a special family time, with each family building and re-building its own traditions.

—It is centered on the birth of Christ who came to identify with the poor, not with those who can give the fanciest gadgets.

—It is a time for people to touch and be touched by each other.

—It is an opportunity to move gently one more step in a journey toward solidarity with the poor.

This last point needs more explanation. One of the things our family and other families have attempted to do is to align our gift-giving with our desire to be part of an empowerment of the economically poor. Many of our gifts come from self-help groups or cooperatives that distribute hand-made craft items from Third World craftspeople, and/or from groups that are working in some way to promote justice in our society.

10. Responses to the culture

One of the biggest obstacles to our attempts at simplifying our lives is the constant message from our culture urging us to buy more, newer, bigger items. Needless to say our children are not immune to these messages. TV is a constant purveyor of these ideas. The following exercise, from a manual called *Television Awareness Training,*[12] is designed to make us more conscious of the messages TV is sending us. We recommend doing it as a family.

TV QUIZ FOR MARTIANS

Watch television for a continuous two-hour stretch.

Pretend you are from Mars: Imagine that what you are seeing on the screen is the only information you have about Americans.

—Spend the first hour watching two half-hour portions of shows.

—Spend the second hour switching the channel selector every five minutes to sample programming at random.

1. Discuss what you have seen. As Martians, what would be your ideas about Americans, judging from the shows and ads you have seen?

—What are women like?

—What are men like?

—What do people do most of the time?

—What is the goal of most Americans?

—What do Americans value highly?

—What do they believe in?

—What are Blacks like? Hispanics? Asian-Americans? Native Americans? Americans of European descent?

—What do people do for pleasure?

2. Now switch your identity back from Martian observers to the Americans who were being observed. Discuss the experience of being observed and the descriptions of you that these "outsiders" gave. How does it feel to be seen and described in that way?

Other strategies for dealing with TV and children vary. One family we know simply does not allow TV watching except for very special occasions. Another family has agreed on a limit of five hours per week. The parents feel that this limit has helped their children (ages ten to sixteen) choose wisely. Our own children do not watch much TV; when they do we try periodically to watch it with them, both to deal with comments and questions about the content of the programs, and to inject some thoughts about the commercials. With older children especially, some more intentional work can be done in terms of an advertising critique—having a family discussion, bringing in ads from magazines, etc.

The Economic Justice Program of the Justice and Peace Center (1016 N. Ninth, Milwaukee, WI 53233) has an excellent program for families and schools on helping us see how children's tastes and "needs" are manipulated by advertising, especially on television. The two films in the program—"Seeing Through Commercials" and "The $6 Billion Sell"—are excellent for family viewing, a parish meeting (PTO, CCD, adult education, other parish groups), or classroom use. "Seeing Through Commercials" is also available for rental from the Institute for Peace & Justice, 2913 Locust St., St. Louis, MO 63103.

Peer pressure to "have" things is truly a force to be reckoned with. In helping children deal with that pressure it is crucial to keep the channels of communication open in order to be regularly aware of what they are facing and how they are choosing to deal with it. St. Louis friends of ours, Ruth and Leroy, tell us that for several years their young teenagers did not want to be seen riding in their old car. Now, however, because the parents (and the old car) are available for transporting teens to games, dances, and so on, the old car has become acceptable again.

Then, once we are more *aware* of the influences of TV, advertising, and peers on our children and on ourselves, we still have to face the question of *action* to bring about change. TV stations and advertisers need to hear from us through letters or phone calls. A family letter to a TV station, for example, can be a good beginning for children in learning how to deal with institutions. A refusal to buy products from a company as a protest against their advertising or marketing policies is another action that the whole family can participate in. Chapter 6 on social action presents further possibilities for family action.

Conclusion

Two points need to be made in conclusion. First, concern about simplifying one's life takes on a different dimension when addressed to the economically poor. Obviously, cutting down is not an issue when you are concerned with survival. We hope some of the suggestions in this chapter will be helpful for families who *have* to live on less as well as families who want to live on less.

Second, there is the question of time. Many suggestions about simplifying our lives are time-consuming, and thus involve a trade-off. What we have found helpful is to do one thing at a time. We feel it is crucial not to be overwhelmed with how much there is to do and how much we are not doing right now. We need to move one step at a time, and to be comfortable with saying to ourselves, "These other ideas may be good things to do, but right now I can't." Further, there is the question of the connection between time and sexism. As is pointed out in Chapter 5 on sex-role stereotyping, time-consuming steps should be shared as much as possible by all family members. The burden of change should not fall on the wife/mother alone.

As an expression of stewardship, a group of Christians put together the following pledge. We offer it as a prayer, and as a way of keeping a vision of what we would like to be. We think some of its commitments will be appropriate for some people, some for others.

THE SHAKERTOWN PLEDGE

Recognizing that the earth and the fullness thereof is a gift from our gracious God, and that we are called to cherish, nurture, and provide loving stewardship for the earth's resources, and recognizing that life itself is a gift, and a call to responsibility, joy, and celebration, I make the following declarations:

1. I declare myself to be a world citizen.
2. I commit myself to lead an ecologically sound life.
3. I commit myself to lead a life of creative simplicity and to share my personal wealth with the world's poor.
4. I commit myself to join with others in reshaping institutions in order to bring about a more just global society in which all people have full access to the needed resources for their physical, emotional, intellectual, and spiritual growth.
5. I commit myself to occupational accountability, and in so doing, I will seek to avoid the creation of products which cause harm to others.
6. I affirm the gift of my body, and commit myself to its proper nourishment and physical well-being.
7. I commit myself to examine continually my relations with others, and to attempt to relate honestly, morally, and lovingly to those around me.
8. I commit myself to personal renewal through prayer, meditation, and study.
9. I commit myself to responsible participation in a community of faith.[13]

CHAPTER 2

NONVIOLENCE IN THE FAMILY

It was a crisp fall Saturday morning several years ago, and I (Jim) was looking forward to the peace of chopping firewood alone in the back yard. But before long I realized I had company.

"I want it!" demanded five-year-old David.

"No!" shouted Theresa, eighteen months younger and half his size.

There in the garage was the classic standoff. David was on the seat of the family's Big Wheel tricycle. Theresa perched defiantly on the front wheel, straining to block his exit.

At first I was angry at their breaking into my chopping and meditating time. I wanted to grab the Big Wheel away from them both and drag them into the house. Some grace intervened, though, and I was able to recall our decision to work at mutual problem-solving and let the children resolve their own conflicts as much as possible.

Well, after two solid minutes of yelling, the children seemed to be at an impasse. At that I intervened. "Doesn't seem like either of you is getting to ride the Big Wheel. Are you happy about that?"

Both answered no.

"Then what could you do so that you could both be happy?" I asked.

After a few seconds David responded, "We could take turns"—then added, "for ten minutes each." (This had been the solution to a similar impasse not long before.) When I said I would be willing to say when ten minutes were up, Theresa volunteered to let David go first.

Sometimes it actually works! Sometimes I remember to give it—the process—and them—the children—a chance.

More on the "how to's" later. First, a word about the "why" of nonviolent or mutual conflict resolution.

Rationale for Practicing Peace

Peace is not the absence of conflict. Conflict is an inevitable fact of daily life—internal, interpersonal, intergroup, and international conflict. Peace consists in creatively dealing with conflict. Peace is the process of working to resolve conflicts in such a way that both sides win, with increased harmony as the outcome of the conflict and its resolution. The resolution is *peace-full* if the participants come to *want* to cooperate more fully and find themselves enabled to do so.

23

This style of parenting (and relating to others in general) is neither permissive nor authoritarian. It is *mutual*. That is, parents and children work together (so the theory goes), with no one winning or losing. Parents do not make all the decisions; but neither do they give in to the children when their own essential needs, values, interests, and responsibilities are at stake.

This ideal is expressed beautifully in Saint Paul's Letter to the Ephesians:

> If we live by the truth and in love, we will grow in all ways into Christ, who is the head by whom the whole body is fitted and joined together, every joint adding its own strength, for each separate part to work according to its function. So the body grows until it has built itself up, in love [Eph. 4:15–16].

The analogy of a body with different but equal parts all working together is quite appropriate for nonviolent conflict resolution. Underlying this chapter is the assumption (not always realized in practice because of our shortcomings) that parents and children are engaged in a cooperative venture. As Rudolf Dreikurs puts it, equality here means that "all members of the family are equal partners in the family, with functions and responsibilities according to their individual capabilities. They have equal status in expressing their ideas, their complaints, their wishes." We are beginning to take seriously his conviction that "the family . . . belongs to all members, and each is required to make some contribution."[1]

We believe, with Saint Paul, both that each of us (including the children) is unique, and that we should be working together to build up the Body of Christ. We see this Body of Christ on two levels: our family body/community and our world body/community. We want, as a family, to build them up together. Part of our working for peace in the world, then, is working to build our family community. If we can experience the possibility of peace—nonviolent conflict resolution—at the family level, then our faith in the possibility of peace and our willingness to work for it at the other levels grows.

The New Testament provides some of the directives for building family community on the principle of peace or nonviolence. For Jesus, authority is to be seen as service (Matt. 20:20–28), and Jesus showed us something of what this means when he washed the feet of his disciples at the Last Supper (John 13). Two beautiful friends of ours, parents of ten children, have translated Jesus' directive in this way:

> This authority which flows through us from God is an *authority of love*. Love permits freedom. Love is demonstrated through service. Love is based on truth. Our delegated power over our children is the power to free them, the power to serve them, the power to teach them the truth. This is the power of love which can flow through us from God.[2]

Saint Paul phrased it in this way: "Be subject to one another out of reverence for Christ" (Eph. 5:21). After instructing children to obey their parents, he speaks to parents: "Parents, don't nag your children, lest they lose heart" (Eph. 6:4). The translation used in our church on Holy Family Sunday, right before New Year's 1980, read "Fathers, don't . . . " Tommy leaned over to me (Jim), smiled, and shook his finger. The Lord had spoken *to me,* and the first New Year's resolution I ever seriously made I made at that moment.

But it is not just because of our interpretation of the Gospel that we have committed ourselves to trying a more cooperative or mutual style of family living and parenting. What Dreikurs, Thomas Gordon, Stephanie Judson, Priscilla Prutzman, and many others have written (see Resources, at the end of the book), we are beginning to experience. In many ways, problem-solving and shared decision-making with the children, and learning the necessary communication skills for this, takes much more time than either permissive or authoritarian approaches. But the payoffs are much bigger. Greater harmony, motivation, efficiency, children and parents sharing their lives with one another, happiness, communication, discovery of one's worth and potential, less need for punishment, and a practical way in which parents "can learn to exert influence instead of authority,"[3] are among the benefits.

On the other hand, as Gordon points out, the more that parental *power* is the basis of attempts to change their children's behavior, the more resistance, hostility, aggression, lying and hidden feelings, blaming others, bullying, needing to win and hating to lose, submission, conformity, and withdrawing are likely to be found in our children.[4]

The final reason for our commitment to a mutual or participatory style of family living is our commitment to peace and justice. We agree with Dreikurs that an essential goal in parenting is the preparation of future citizens—in our words, proclaimers of the Gospel and thus agents for social change. As Sadie Dreikurs put it after her husband's death:

> Unless children, at the earliest age, experience their own strength and a feeling of belonging, the opportunity for achieving the fullest measure of freedom with responsibility is lost. Once children become full partners in their family, the foundation of their future life is established, and they become contributing members of their school and society. Peoples' potential can only be realized to its fullest when all human beings are confident of their worth to the society in which they live.[5]

Basic Ingredients in Building Family Community

An affirming, cooperative, accepting family environment

All persons have the physiological and psychological potential for violent behavior. But we believe that those who actually resort to violence are people who have learned violence. Unfortunately, in our society as a whole and in many of the families in our society, it is easy to learn violence. Winning and being "number one" are all-important. Seven-year-old boys are rewarded with money for "drawing blood" in a football game. Parents yell and hit and thus so do siblings. Verbal put-downs are common and often give status. The "frontier ethic" is alive and well and flourishing in the United States.

But we believe that children can also learn nonviolence. However, the experience of the educators at the Children's Creative Response to Conflict Program has led them to the conclusion that nonviolence *cannot* be learned as a series of *techniques* divorced from a nonviolent environment. Only in an environment that is more and more cooperative and affirming will children learn nonviolent conflict-resolution skills. We use the phrase "more and more" here to indicate our own only too clear realization that parents are not perfect, that fights will still happen, and that learning nonviolence is a life-long process through many a failure.

In trying to live more nonviolently, we do not believe we are preparing our children to live in an unreal world. "Street skills" or "survival skills" are important. But we are also concerned that the children learn a second set of skills, which they can improve by testing them out in the so-called real world, as well as at home, and talk with us about the difficulties involved.

So how do we build this affirming, cooperative, accepting environment? Examples are legion, and every family has its own special ones.

Affirmation: One of us tries to look over the children's schoolwork quickly when they come home or right before dinner. Positive comments should prevail over negative ones, though constructive criticism is also in order (as much from them as from us).

Conscious affirmation of one another sometimes happens at mealtimes or occasionally in the car. Especially after a string of meals at which we seem to be more conscious of the children's table manners than of their person, we will ask each person to say one thing he or she likes about each family member, or one thing each person is good at. Sometimes we ask each other what our favorite foods, songs, and the like, are, or what have been our favorite moments of the day.

"Affirmation claps" are another part of our family's repertoire. Family members, and especially others, are affirmed in their specialness to us by "double claps," "triple claps," and so on, depending on how special the person or experience has been for the children. It is quick, active, fun, and—best of all—something the children taught us. Prutzman's *Friendly Classroom for a Small Planet* (see Resources) is a source of many other such possibilities, including "Affirmation Valentines," in which we write reasons we love one another.

Physical affection helps too. Lots of it. Bedtime and as the children leave for school are regular times for us. Holding hands as we pray before meals increases physical contact and at least symbolizes caring, although it does not always occasion feelings of affection among the children! (Be patient, we keep reminding ourselves.)

Also important here, especially when the number of children in the family increases, is to have some time with each child individually. All parents know how much more enjoyable our children often are when they are with us alone. They feel special and affirmed. And the more we enjoy them, the more we are willing to persevere in the physically and emotionally draining vocation of parenthood.

In addition to affirming one another individually, we occasionally affirm ourselves as a family. If we celebrate our unity, we are more willing to work together. Having a special family place where we celebrate our being together helps us. For us, there are two such places—both of them picnic spots. The winter spot is on the floor in front of our fireplace, with a picnic tablecloth and dinner. The other special place is in a park, where we now go for our first meal back home after our long summer trips.

Family game nights, wrestling in the living room, the kids hopping into bed with us in the morning (sometimes), are all family affirmations as well as fun. Despite my residual rigidity, we are experiencing the truth of Elise Boulding's observation that "playfulness, openness and love go together. So do rigidity and violence."

Something we learned from *Family Adventures Toward Shalom*[6] and have adapted for ourselves is keeping our "family story." Using photographs and other mementos, we are recording our family life in a scrapbook, year by year. Once we catch up with the present, we plan to make this an annual family afternoon New Year's Eve celebration—finding the items that best capture the year for us as a family. Prayers of thanksgiving and plans for the coming year will probably be included.

Part of an affirming environment is an air of acceptance. Nonviolence is not bred in an environment where criticism overshadows acceptance. As I read Charlie Shedd's *Promises to Peter*[7] (his son), I was struck by three of his promises. Having a real streak of non-acceptance or rigidity in myself, I also felt judged, particularly by the first of the three.

I promise you that I will never say "no" if I can possibly say "yes."
I pledge that I will really be with you when I am with you.
I pledge you also that I will try to see things from a child's point of view.

Minimize the "no's" and the demands, and maximize the areas of self-governance, he says.

An affirmative environment is more than likely a cooperative one too. Violence is nurtured by excessive competition. Nonviolence, on the other hand, springs from cooperation. Families have numerous opportunities to promote a cooperative environment at home. Some family chores require (or can be structured to require) more than one person to do them. Sometimes it is two or more of the children sharing the task—emptying wastebaskets and raking leaves work best when one person holds the bag while the other fills it. Sometimes a parent can work with the children—Theresa and I doing the dishes, David and Kathy baking.

Adult activities can often include one or more of the children—trips to the hardware store, the grocery store, the recycling center. Reading a story to a couple of the children at the same time, involving David as well as Theresa in painting her dollhouse, are examples of how we try to balance time with the children together along with time with them individually. Sometimes in family games we play as teams.

Encouraging the children to help each other, teach each other skills, is still another area. Tommy occasionally will help David with his reading. Theresa consented to David's helping her learn to ride her bike. Some "share-toys" along with the personal individual toys can encourage cooperation. Chapter 1 on stewardship examines this idea more fully.

Before proceeding to the specific skills involved in nonviolent conflict resolution, it might be good to look at your own family environment and try to answer the following questions:[8]
—Is the mood of your family a cooperative one? Is it relaxed or tense?
—Do you feel good about yourselves and others?
—Do you listen to one another?
—Do all communicate clearly?
—Do you have fun together? Enjoy being home?
—How do you generally resolve conflicts?

Nonviolent communication skills

Numerous books have been written on why and how to communicate nonviolently. Here we can only highlight what we have found worthwhile from our own experience and from reading generally helpful books like Gordon's *Parent Effectiveness Training* (see Resources). Here are three communication skills and principles we see as important for nonviolent conflict resolution.

1. Expressing wants in clear action-terms. We agree with Gordon on the importance of sending what he calls "I-messages" rather than "you-messages," and of referring to specific behavior rather than making general judgments. Thus if I have a problem with someone's behavior, then I need to name it as my problem, and name it in clear action-terms. Compare the following statements:
—"Hey, I can't concentrate. Why don't you think about anybody but yourself? I want some consideration around here!"
—"I'm trying to read, but I can't concentrate with the disco records on that loud. Can you turn it down, or put on some soft music, or wait a half-hour until I finish?"
Here, both complaints state my need. But the second offers possible solutions rather than merely stating my need and requiring the child to generate a solution; and it avoids the put-down and destructiveness the first statement falls into with its "you-message" and its call for "consideration" (whatever that might mean). The "I-message," if expressed in a voice and with words

that fit, invites a response rather than a counter-attack! Tommy will now figure that I am probably willing to hear *his* wants, and he will more likely state them less defensively in his response. Now with my problem clearly named, the way is open to our finding a mutually agreeable solution.

2. *Expressing our feelings honestly, along with our wants.* But often our feelings are more important than our wants, and need to be expressed as clearly, honestly, and gently as we can. Compare:

—"Hey, get in here and clean up your room! You're really dependable! You can't even remember your own agreements. You want to make us late for Grandma's?"

—"I'm really disappointed. I thought we had an agreement where you'd clean your room on Saturday morning before going outside. I want you to come in and clean it now, since we're leaving for Grandma's in thirty minutes."

In the second statement, the feeling is named (disappointment) and the reason for it is given. In the first statement, besides the sarcastic, blaming tone, a feeling is not named—although anger is clearly the feeling communicated! Of course, there are times when the primary feeling *is* anger and this should then be stated. Here, however, the primary feeling is disappointment. The honest statement of our disappointment can be an invitation to growth for the other person. Communicating the secondary feeling, anger, as primary, is unnecessary and invites resentment.

Further, unless the feelings are expressed and understood, it may be impossible to deal with the wants. Hiding our feelings can cause resentment and can ultimately lead to violence. As Kathy and I become more comfortable with and skillful in expressing our negative feelings, we are trying to help the children grow in the same way. Many couples have recommended sharing their feelings and working through their conflicts occasionally in front of the children.

Often we can speak to the children's own feelings, naming those feelings with them: "You're feeling angry right now, aren't you?" This is where the next skill comes in.

3. *Active listening.* This expression of Thomas Gordon's refers to a kind of listening and response that does not judge, ridicule, praise, warn, order, or the like. Instead, the listener tries to feed back or paraphrase the feeling(s) and want(s) of the speaker, checking out the accuracy of the hearing. With children, this is also a way of helping them clarify their own feelings and wants. "You'd like me to stop yelling at you when I'm mad, is that right?" or "You're saying you were bored the last time we went to the demonstration at General Dynamics because there weren't any other children there?"

We are learning that the more we listen without judging, as hard as it is to do, the more we help our children accept their feelings, improve their own problem-solving ability, increase their willingness to listen to us, and expand the warmth and empathy in all of us. As Gordon points out, such listening requires certain attitudes: a desire to listen and be helpful, an acceptance of others' feelings and separateness, and a trust in their ability to solve problems.

Family meetings offer us a weekly chance to learn these skills, but dozens of other opportunities are available daily, especially at mealtimes and after school. We try to take turns talking at meals, making sure the older children do not drown out the younger ones. In conflict situations we try to help them hear one another's wants: "David, do you know why Theresa is so angry with you? Can you tell him, Theresa?" If she does, we might then ask, "David, do you understand what she said? Can you tell me?"

The importance of listening, as far as peace and justice is concerned, is expressed by Elise Boulding:

> Many of the young people in these [social change] communities had the experience of being listened to and respected when they were children. They developed a sense that their thoughts and actions would make a difference. Probably in the childhood of every activist peacemaker there were one or many experiences of being trusted and attended to by an adult. Such experiences build up a reservoir of competence and inner security that makes it possible to take risks on behalf of what one believes.[9]

Nonviolent conflict resolution

The importance of active listening in nonviolent conflict resolution was brought home to me anew just recently. Nine-year-old Tommy and his friend Sean headed down to the basement to play, with seven-year-old David close behind, apparently to check on the security of his things. Sure enough, I heard the rattling of the hubcap David had found earlier. Loud voices soon joined the rattling, followed shortly by cries. I appeared, and found a punched nine-year-old and a bitten seven-year-old, each telling me the hubcap was his.

Sean was asked to leave for a while, and Tommy and David were sent to separate rooms to calm down. I went to each to hear his feelings and his side of the story (without comment—ordinarily I would have had a number of choice comments, but I had literally just been reading Gordon's chapter on active listening). In five minutes they said they were ready to talk about it. So I put them in their room with instructions to come to some agreement they both could live with and report it to me; then they could go back to play. Tommy protested briefly that he wanted to play first, but I said no.

The first six exchanges I heard as I walked down the stairs were remarkably similar: "It's mine!" "No, it's mine!" "No, it's mine!" "I said it's mine!" "I found it first!" "No, I found it first!" I did decide to intervene now, to remind them that they had to agree on how to play with the hubcap before they could resume playing. Well, in less than ten minutes Tommy was walking out the front door. I asked him to explain their agreement. He did. Then I asked David to explain it. He said it was just as Tommy had said. The agreement sounded pretty elaborate—where the hubcap would be kept, who could play with it first, who could play with it when the other didn't want it, what would happen if it were taken out of the drawer without consulting the other. But the complexity of the agreement seemed to boggle only my feeble brain. The boys seemed fine and were off to play.

Because of this and other experiences, we are coming to agree with the advice of friends, as well as of experts like Gordon, on a parent's role in child-child conflicts. Expressed as a series of principles or steps, this advice might be digested as follows.

1. Stay out of child-child conflicts altogether if possible. Intervene only if someone is getting hurt or your own needs are being interfered with by the conflict.

2. Intervene in such a way as to enable the children to resolve the conflict themselves.

Jerry and Martha, friends of ours with five children, have applied these principles somewhat as in our own hubcap incident. When their twelve-year-old and nine-year-old sons are fighting, tempers are usually very high. So the boys are separated for five minutes, to calm down and find possible solutions. Then they are brought together to arrive at an actual solution. If they cannot find one, then a parent imposes one. Because they generally do not like the solutions imposed, more often than not they find their own.

Other friends of ours, Mike and Barbara, are very clear with their five children, ranging in age from five to fifteen: "Solve your conflicts yourselves. If you cannot, then bring them to the weekly family meeting, where the whole family can help. If you absolutely cannot wait until then, then one of us will serve as a mediator." Rarely has either of them had to be summoned for mediator duty, once family meetings became weekly.

Problem-solving in parent-child conflicts is another matter. We agree with Gordon that there are three basic ways of dealing with most parent-child conflicts: modifying the environment, changing ourselves, and problem-solving with the children.

1. *Modifying the environment.*[10] Sometimes conflicts can be reduced and mutual enjoyment increased by modifying the environment. *Enriching* the environment (providing more stimuli) encourages creativity and reduces boredom and conflicts. *Impoverishing* the environment, like calming children down before bedtime, can also reduce conflicts. *Simplifying* the environment, that is, making it easier for children to do things without causing problems, like using spill-proof cups, can help too. *Restricting* the environment, for example by confining loud indoor play to the basement, will often help considerably, as does *child-proofing* the environment: giving a one-year-old an old magazine to tear up rather than one we are still reading is an example of child-proofing by substituting one activity for another. *Planning ahead* with children and preparing them for changes also helps: if the children realize that Saturday afternoon and evening will be taken up by visiting

Grandma, they will be more likely to complete their chores on Saturday morning without a hassle. Gordon adds a note with which Kathy and I agree, although we do not usually remember to implement it: as the children get older, modifications in the home environment should be by mutual decisions whenever possible. The home belongs to the children as well as to the parents.

2. *Changing ourselves.* Expanding the possibilities of nonviolent conflict resolution by changing ourselves is a very real possibility for all of us. For Kathy and me this has come to mean four things. First, checking with other parents and with teachers, along with an occasional parenting book, is helping us form more realistic expectations of our children. Talking with parents of older children has helped us get a longer-term perspective on our children. Current problems often seem less monumental when viewed in relation to the problems of adolescents. Usually we feel more relaxed after such discussions and are a little more easy-going with our children.

Second, doing enjoyable things with the children balances the inevitable negative aspects of living with them. We want to increase our positive feelings about the children. "Solutions" with negative feelings prevailing are not *non-violent* conflict resolutions for us as a family. More and more we are looking for experiences we can share which we enjoy as much as the children do. It is making a real difference for us.

Third, we are getting clearer about our own wants, and doing more things that give *us* real satisfaction. The more we feel positive about ourselves individually, the more positive we are in relation to the children. Not long ago I found myself saying, "Damn it, if I can't find time for so many of the things I want, I'll at least get you kids to do what I want!"—not exactly a prescription for mutual problem-solving. I decided then and there to change my own situation, to make time for my guitar, poetry, jogging, and friends, so that the children would not continue to suffer from my frustrations.

Last, and likewise, the more Kathy and I enjoy each other, the more positive and open we are to the children. If we want to be good for our children we had better be good for each other. Without this critical link the whole chain of parenting for peace and justice comes apart.

3. *Mutual problem-solving with the children.* Obviously, even after minimizing conflicts by modifying the environment and by modifying ourselves, parent-child conflicts occur daily. More and more of these, particularly the recurring conflicts, we—the children as well as ourselves—are bringing to our weekly family meeting. Other parent-child conflicts need to be dealt with on the spot.

Although we often short-cut the process, we recommend these steps as a systematic way of problem-solving as a family, of coming to a consensus.

Step 1. Name the problem or conflict clearly. That is, what are the conflicting needs? Expressing feelings as well as wants, and "active listening," are important aspects of this step. Each participant in the conflict needs to feel heard and understood.

Step 2. Brainstorm alternatives. Everyone's idea is listened to. (We do not allow evaluation yet, like "that's a stupid idea!")

Step 3. Evaluate the alternatives. Here is where short-cuts are often taken; younger children do not have the capacity for staying with a process for a long time. Kathy and I often kibbitz a little here—helping one or more of the children see how their needs will be met by someone else's suggestions, or how that suggestion could be modified slightly to meet other's needs.

Step 4. Poll the group to see if we have found an alternative that everyone can accept.

Step 5. Decide how to implement the solution. Who is responsible for which tasks, and (where applicable) when we will evaluate how well the solution is working?

Are there limits to our problem-solving with children? For what issues is problem-solving appropriate? At what ages? How much should the children be allowed to participate? Definitely there are limits. The limits are the values and needs of each family member, including the parents. As the children get older and more verbal, we are finding few if any issues involving the children that are inappropriate for mutual decision-making.

Nutrition is a basic concern of parents. Do we allow our children to eat whatever they want whenever they want it? No. As we mentioned in Chapter 1, we decided as a family when the children were eight, six, and four years old that they would choose their after-school snacks once a week for the whole week, and that the snacks had to be nutritious and low in sugar content.

Not that it always works smoothly. As I was writing the lines just above, the children came home from school. David and Theresa asked if they could go to the neighborhood store and buy some candy with their own money. "We haven't gone in two weeks," David pleaded, knowing his chances were not very good. When I asked pointedly whether they had spent some money for treats at a church movie the day before, tears formed in David's eyes. "I knew you'd say no!"

"No, David, let's talk about it. We're going to Cincinnati in two days on a special trip."

"Right," he retorted, "and we won't get to spend any money then either."

Recalling last week was Valentine's and the children had had their fill of candy (in our estimation, that is), I launched into our "cavities-and-dentist-bills" speech, and ended up with, "No, David, I think more candy today is just too much candy. What's the snack today?" "Raisins," he mumbled. "How about if you get some peanuts and raisins both, as a special treat?"

The motion seemed to die for lack of a second, but suddenly David was up in the kitchen cabinet getting two bowls and the bag of peanuts. "Everybody gets twenty peanuts, then," he proclaimed. "OK," said I, and, spotting two tiny candy hearts from Valentine's Day, I asked if the children would like to have them too. Simultaneous smiles indicated that we had stumbled on a truly acceptable solution.

It took about eight minutes to complete the process—eight minutes I do not often have the patience or flexibility to find. (But how could I go back to writing about shared decision-making without taking the time?)

Clothes have been a more difficult area, one that has required occasional re-negotiation. Parents who problem-solve with their children know that even the best solutions do not work forever. Both the children and we want their areas of self-governance to increase, but there are some limits. T-shirts plus long-sleeved shirts are winter requirements. Clean socks and underwear are daily musts. Clean clothes for school and church are also required.

But what *constitutes* "clean" has been a matter of contention. Our previous rule of different clothes each day has been modified by mutual decision. If any child (generally David) wants to wear clothes a second or third day (the new limit), he inspects them with one of us for cleanliness. Soon, we hope such monitoring, as well as checking their clothes for some minimal style and color matching, will no longer be necessary. But it will take patience, because one has to stay with such things for months and sometimes years.

For examples of increasing self-governance with older children, we recommend Charlie Shedd's captivating book about the Shedd family, *Promises to Peter.* For activities to develop nonviolent conflict resolution skills in younger children, Priscilla Prutzman's *Friendly Classroom for a Small Planet* and Stephanie Judson's *Nonviolence and Children* are excellent. (See Resources.)

Family meeting: regular shared decision-making

Like many other families, we are finding our weekly family meeting to be the main focus of our efforts at shared decision-making and problem-solving. Here everyone is an equal. Here permission has clearly been given to bring complaints and conflicts to the surface. Here there is the time needed for many of those issues that are not resolved well or mutually when everyone is on the run. Here, then, is a weekly class on nonviolence for all of us. And here there is the symbol as well as the reality of the unity of our family—the Body of Christ assembled, working together to build up its unity.

1. Definition and components. After having a number of family meetings, we came across a book called *Family Council.* (See Resources.) What Dreikurs wrote there confirmed our own experience with family meetings. His definition of a "family council" (our family meeting) embodies the components we think essential. First the definition, then some of the key components.

The group shall have regularly scheduled meetings and operate under rules agreed upon in advance. The meeting shall be an open forum at which all family members can speak without interruption, with freedom of expression, without fear of consequences, and without regard for age or status. Its deliberations result in decisions only when all members present agree—that is, come to a common understanding.[11]

a. Regularly scheduled. At first we held our family meetings only every few months. But they became monthly, then weekly. Their frequency increased as the children got older and wanted to participate, as the agenda multiplied, and as the parents' willingness to meet deepened.

A regularly scheduled time is important for several reasons. First, schedules can be cleared more easily. Especially as the children get older, the family should choose the time that best fits everyone's schedule. Second, family members are more likely to plan to bring issues to a family meeting when they know there will be one, and when.

Time and place should be geared to maximize results. A place and time where people are relaxed is better than one where they are tense or distracted. Dinnertime works well for us and others. If people are tense, sometimes it helps to begin with something we call "excitement sharing"—something funny or interesting that happened to each person that day or during the past few days. We have also found it helpful if the family meeting is followed by a "fun" event—a family game, or special TV show, or trip to an ice cream parlor. It puts the meeting experience into an enjoyable, community-building context. This often increases the quality of the meeting.

b. Rules agreed upon in advance. The rules we have started with are very simple. Take turns talking, listen when others talk, talk about one item at a time, no voting, and anyone can put any item on the agenda. The only other rule is to stay with the present rules for a while or until the children specifically request a change. Sometime in the future, unless the children beat us to it, we will raise the question of rotating leaders. For now, though, we want the children simply to experience the process under our leadership.

The process we use for each item is essentially the same as that outlined on pages 32–33.

Step 1. The person who has put a particular item on the agenda is asked to explain it. Others may only ask clarifying questions.

Step 2. (If necessary) If the person raising the issue has not suggested a change or solution, he or she is asked to propose one.

Step 3. Others are asked for other possible solutions. (Sometimes everyone likes the one suggested at the beginning.)

The final three steps are (4) evaluating the alternatives, (5) deciding on one, and (6) working out a plan to implement it.

An example of how this has worked in practice for us:

An item appeared on the agenda listed as "naps."

Kathy: "Whose item is 'naps' "?

David: "Mine."

Kathy: "What do you want to say about naps?"

David: "No more naps! We're old enough now!"

Theresa: "But what if we want to stay up late sometime, when we go out or have a TV party?"

Jim (glancing at Kathy with delighted surprise): "That's a good point, Theresa. What should we do on those days?"

After a number of comments and suggestions had been heard, Jim suggested naps on the day of or day after a late night out. Theresa, David, and Tommy all agreed. Now, two months later, one or more of the children occasionally ask to take a nap on the weekend so that they can stay up late!

c. Open forum. Each person is free to speak without interruption, without being judged. Sometimes families experience the problem of one or more members dominating or talking for long periods of time. The best way to handle this (or any other source of dissatisfaction) is to evaluate the family meetings periodically. Each family member shares what he or she likes about the family meetings and what he or she would like to see done differently. Those changes are made which everyone agrees to.

Open forum means open agenda, too. Any family member can put any item on the agenda. To promote this openness, we tape the agenda to the wall of our breakfast room where we hold our family meetings. We try to get it up a day before the meeting to give everyone ample time to add items.

d. Consensus decisions. Although the children still suggest it at times, we have avoided voting altogether. Majority rule may be the "American Way," but it is less peaceful and community-building than consensus decision-making. There are losers in a majority-rule vote. Split decisions can some-times mean tiny splits in a family. Sometimes, though, we have modified our consensus approach; for instance, if there is not total agreement on what game to play or where to go for dinner, then we sometimes decide by consen-sus to rotate who gets to choose for the whole family.

2. Ways of encouraging the children's participation. In addition to combin-ing the family meeting with some kind of fun event, there are ways of holding the meeting itself so as to encourage the children's participation and every-one's good feelings.

a. Agenda items. It is important to include items other than problems. Otherwise, the spirit tends to be a little negative. Allowances are distributed at our family meetings. Some families settle their weekly schedule and trans-portation needs as part of the family meeting. Discussing family purchases is another generally creative item. At least once a month, we add two items called "family fun" and "family service." Both are enjoyable and creative. Here we decide on some special "fun" thing that does not cost much that we can do as a family. Then we decide on some way we can serve others and work for justice as a family. (See Chapter 6.)

Another thing we do is to make sure at least some of the children's agenda items are considered early in the meeting. We want them to see that the process can work for their needs as well as ours. In this vein, we encourage the children to bring personal problems to the family meeting if they want help from others.

Actually, Tommy was the one who initiated it. He was not able to stop sniffing. It was driving all of us crazy! When it became a problem at school, too, he decided to ask for help. It was a beautiful experience.

Kathy: "What did you want to say about 'sniffing'?"

Tommy: "I know you said it was my problem and I should figure out what to do about it, but I just thought you might have some ideas for me."

Kathy (astonished): "You want some ideas on how to stop, Tommy?"

Tommy: "Yes."

We brainstormed possibilities for a few minutes and came to a point system—one point for every time period at home (a meal, the hour before dinner, the hour after dinner, etc.) during which there were no sniffs; one-half point for only one sniff; no points for more than one sniff. The whole school day counted as one time period and Tommy was the judge. He would record the points and get a treat everytime he got five points. That it worked was fine. That Tommy thought to ask the family's help was wonderful!

b. How the items are handled. There are other ways to encourage the genuine participation of the children. One way is to exclude punishments where possible. For example, we proposed discussing how to encourage the boys to lift the toilet seat when they urinated. (You see, no real issues are excluded and this was a real issue). David suggested a five-cent fine for every time he or Tommy forgot. This would be in addition to making and posting signs next to each toilet and David and Tommy taking turns cleaning their toilets. But Kathy and I did not want a negative consequence involved right away. Thus we suggested that we see how it went for a week without the fines; if it was not working, then we would be willing to consider fines the next week. At other times, negative consequences seemed necessary; in such cases we found it worked best if they were determined together by consensus.

Not scolding (or, more realistically in my case, reducing the amount of scolding) between meetings for not doing what was agreed upon at previous family meetings is another help; bringing up the issue at the next family meeting where it can be handled more democratically is still further help. The whole climate of the house changes. And when each of us knows we have a regular forum for raising behavioral problems, we do not feel compelled to "sound off" quite so often.

But even with all these efforts, Dreikurs cautions us to have realistic expectations. Acknowledging the lack of societal supports, he states that this whole endeavor "requires cooperation on the part of all. It requires a shift in roles by all family members. . . . In the competitive society in which we live, cooperation is hard to achieve, but it can develop."[12]

Discipline: consequences and punishments

This is the most difficult aspect of nonviolent child-raising for us and the most difficult part of this chapter to write. First, it is hard to put into a few pages the emotions and experiences of years, when whole books have been written on the subject. Second, every parent knows how difficult it is to try to balance affirmation and correction, freedom and firmness, especially when the parents are under stress themselves. Child abuse is a serious problem in our society. Thus we have to find ways of expanding the possibilities of what might be called "nonviolent discipline."

For us, nonviolent discipline means several things. First, as much as possible (which, for us, now may be about one-third of the time) we try to bring

issues requiring discipline to our family meeting. Here, the children participate in deciding the consequences of continuing unacceptable behavior. As I
have said, we try to make punishments a last resort. The first resort is to try to
get the children to identify ways in which we can help them *remember* to carry
out the desired behavior (like signs by the toilet seats, or a check list
for Tommy to help him remember his morning chores). If these fail, *then*
some kind of negative consequence is decided upon. For instance, it was
a group decision to levy a five-cent fine for each chore not done on time,
payable out of the allowances to be distributed at the next family meeting.

Well and good, but how about all those other times where correction is
needed?

Now that the children are getting older, more reasoning is possible. Sometimes we are able to arrive at the negative consequence together. "I'm really
frustrated, David, nothing seems to work about your getting dressed. What
can we do about it?"

More often, though, we find ourselves imposing a punishment. In these
situations, we try (generally) to find one that is immediate and is as close to a
"natural consequence" of the behavior as possible. Coming home late for
dinner may mean missing part or all of dinner. Not telling us they were at a
friend's house, or getting in trouble at a friend's house, may mean not being
allowed to go to that friend's house the next day or week. Breaking a brother's
toy means paying for it or finding an acceptable substitute from one's own
toy supply.

But what about those many run-ins that parents and children have—in the
store, at home, in someone else's home—in the form of tantrums or other
disruptive, annoying, or "smart" behaviors that little ones are so good at and
which drive parents crazy? Here are several thoughts, which we preface with
a confession that while we have come a long way, we have a long way yet to go
in doing what we are suggesting.

—Charlie Shedd's advice makes sense to us: "Whenever we discipline our
children, it should be for them and not for us."[13] By this he means asking
ourselves several questions: Do I care too much about what others think? Do
I want things to be my way too much? Am I extra careful when I'm down or
tired?

—If children are unwilling to cooperate, sometimes it is best simply to
remove them from the situation until they decide to cooperate. Sending them
or removing them to their room can be done without shouting at them,
though many times I have found myself combining the two.

—When I have lost my cool, especially when the children were younger,
and I spanked them, I have tried to go back as soon as possible and apologize
and hug them and explain how frustrated I was. There were a couple of years
when I was so impatient that my hope for the children's psychic well-being
hinged on their sensing the love in my hugs. What we mentioned earlier about
feeling good about ourselves individually and about ourselves as a couple is

crucial here. Often children are the targets of parental frustrations that have nothing to do with them.

Finally, then, a word about corporal punishment. It is a rare parent who has never spanked or slapped a child. But, as someone who has "been there," I would counsel caution about corporal punishment. Two comments stand out in my mind.

Recently a father shared this reflection with us: "I'm sure that my inability to control my temper is the biggest factor in our kids' learning violence."

Only a few weeks before, we had challenged Tommy about his yelling and fighting with David. His frustrated rejoinder was, "I just can't seem to do it any other way." That hit me right between the eyes. For probably two years or more I had been unable consistently to find nonviolent alternatives in my own dealings with David. The question is there: What are we teaching our children when we resort to physical or verbal violence with them?

More and more, Kathy and I are coming to agree with the findings of a recent "Gilmartin Report" on the effects of regular spanking. We found an outline in an excellent newsletter for parents, *For Parents: A Newsletter for Family Enrichment:*

1. Children who are often spanked tend to be more quiet, less articulate, and more sullen.

2. Spanking tends to create nervousness and slow down learning.

3. Harsh physical and psychological punishment leads to social distance among family members. When social distance increases, honest communication decreases.

4. Frequent use of physical punishment is strongly associated with the development of a low self-image in children.

5. Violence begets violence. Physical punishment for fighting simply does not teach kids to stop fighting.

6. Spanking is related to chronic passivity in children.

7. Children who are controlled through being spanked develop an overdependence on external control. They become followers, always dependent on the watchful eyes of an overseer.[14]

Conclusion

Underlying the values and suggestions in this chapter is a vision of children, of our role as parents, and of God's love that is expressed in a special way in Kahlil Gibran's reflection "On Children" in *The Prophet.* Every once in a while we return to this passage to regain that vision.[15]

Your children are not your children.
They are the sons and daughters of Life's longing for itself.
They come through you but not from you,
And though they are with you, yet they belong not to you. . . .

You are the bows from which your children as living arrows are sent
forth.
The archer sees the mark upon the path of the infinite,
and He bends you with His might that His arrows may go swift and far.
Let your bending in the archer's hand be for gladness;
For even as He loves the arrow that flies,
so He loves also the bow that is stable.

CHAPTER 3

HELPING CHILDREN DEAL WITH VIOLENCE IN OUR WORLD

The children and I (Kathy) were driving to a shopping center. On the way we passed the offices and plant of an aircraft manufacturer in our area, whose main business was in military contracts. The children asked what kind of work people did there.

In answering their questions, I included my opinion about the defense industry. I said I wished a company like this would use more of its resources making commercial airplanes and other peace-related items. I said I wished they did not make bombers and fighter planes.

The responses of Tommy and David were very straightforward: "We have to have bombs! We have to be able to get the enemy so they can't get us. Bombs will help us fight!"

As we talked further, I became very aware of two underlying themes in what they were saying: (1) they saw the world with pretty much of an "us against them" view; (2) they had little grasp of the *totality* of the destructiveness of war. They felt that somehow bombs would pick out the "bad people." It had not occurred to them that bombs kill children.

This conversation represented only "the tip of the iceberg"; yet in another sense it was the whole iceberg, on a micro-scale. How do we as parents explain violence in our world to our children? How do we help them understand and cope with all these manifestations of violence, from the bully down the street to the total destructiveness of a nuclear bomb? How do we help them think in terms of *cooperation* with peoples around the world, instead of dealing with people out of a fear-driven sense of competition?

Rationale for Dedication to World Peace

"To work for peace is the concern of all individuals and of all peoples. And because everyone is endowed with a heart and with reason and has been made in the image of God, he or she is capable of the effort of truth and sincerity which strengthens peace" (Pope John Paul II, 1980).[1]

The call to be peacemakers is certainly not a new one. The Old Testament prophets called the people of their time to respond to Yahweh's call for peace. And they foretold the mission of the Savior, to be a deliverer of peace and

41

justice. Zechariah tells the people, "You must love truth and peace" (8:18), and "these are the things you should do: Speak the truth to one another. In the courts give real justice—the kind that brings peace" (8:16). And Isaiah looks to the coming of the Messiah: "He will wield authority over the nations and adjudicate between many peoples, they will hammer their swords into plowshares, their spears into sickles. Nation will not lift sword against nation, there will be no more training for war" (Isa. 2:4–5).

Then Christ confirmed the prophets' call. The mission and message of Christ was and is one of love, not hate, justice, not oppression, peace, not war. "Happy are the peacemakers: they shall be called the children of God" (Matt. 5:9). And he leaves us with a legacy of peace—"Peace is what I leave with you; it is my own peace that I give you" (John 14:27). Paul exhorted the newly forming Christian community, "Do everything possible on your part to live in peace with everybody" (Rom. 12:18). And "Do your best to preserve the unity which the Spirit gives by means of the peace that binds you together" (Eph. 4:3).

Violent resolution of conflict, and war itself, certainly does not "preserve the unity which the Spirit gives." The churches have called their people to work for an end to war. Some Christian groups have done this for centuries. Others have become more outspoken in recent years as the horrors of war have become more obvious. The Quakers issued this position on war as long ago as 1660:

> We utterly deny all outward wars and strife, and fightings with outward weapons, for any end, or under any pretense whatsoever; this is our testimony to the whole world. . . . The Spirit of Christ, by which we are guided, is not changeable, so as once to command us from a thing as evil, and again to move unto it; and we certainly know, and testify to the world, that the Spirit of Christ, which leads us into all truth, will never move us to fight and war against any man with outward weapons, neither for the Kingdom of Christ nor for the kingdoms of this world. . . . Therefore, we cannot learn war any more.[2]

The last line, "We cannot learn war any more," speaks to us as parents. Are our children "learning war"? Are we *teaching them war*? What can we do to teach them peace? Vatican Council II put it this way: "Those who are dedicated to the work of education, particularly to the young, or who mold public opinion, should regard as their most weighty task the effort to instruct all in fresh sentiments of peace."[3] Eleanor Roosevelt put it this way: "It isn't enough to talk about peace. One must believe in it. And it isn't enough to believe in it. One must work at it."[4] It is the task of this chapter to suggest some ways to "work at it" within our families.

We see three broad goals to be set in helping children deal with violence in our world:

1. To help children understand and cope with violence in their immediate world and see alternatives to that violence.

2. To grow in an understanding of the "war mentality" in our culture and find ways to circumvent it in our families.

3. To explore ways to build a mentality of global interdependence within our families.

We want to examine the meaning of each one of these goals, as well as suggest specific strategies to implement them.

Violence in the Community

Children encounter violence and the use of force in their everyday world. For some children this encounter is occasional, for others it is constant. Seemingly unprovoked attacks by other children, violent behavior resulting from drug or alcohol abuse, street crime, some police practices, and conditions in most prisons are all part of our society and therefore part of our children's lives. How do we help our children deal with an influence potentially so destructive for them?

First of all, there is the question of children being able to deal with the sometimes overly aggressive behavior of other children. Do we tell our children to hit back when someone hits them? What do we say about fighting? Chapter 2 on nonviolent conflict resolution lays the basis for children's developing the skills to get their own needs met without having to resort to violent behavior. We have always felt it is essential for our children to have a repertoire of ways to assert themselves and attempt to solve their conflicts. If they only know how to fight, we fear they will find themselves getting hurt or hurting someone else and still not solving the problem.

However, there have been a few times when one of the children was being intimidated by another child to a point where we felt it was necessary to say, "If you have tried everything else and it hasn't worked, then you may have to hit back." And for some children, being able to "hit back" effectively may simply be a matter of survival. But even in these cases, the development of other conflict resolution skills is essential.

Besides helping our children to make decisions about fighting, there is another element in the matter of handling aggression from others. That element is an attempt to understand the reasons for another's actions. Several years ago friends of ours told us about their daughter Anne, then ten years old, who had been repeatedly struck by another child on the way to school. Anne was frightened, but she was also mystified. She could not imagine why the other girl would want to hurt her. Anne's parents used this opportunity to introduce her to some deeper underlying societal conditions that are sometimes causes for violent behavior. The other child lived "on the wrong side of the tracks." They drove through the girl's neighborhood with Anne one day, and past her home. Anne could see that the other girl was poor. Although she said to her parents, "You don't have to be mean just because you're poor"— and there is no denying the truth of that statement—Anne also indicated that she could see that life was not too easy for the other girl.

What Anne's parents were doing, without labeling it as such, was to begin the explanation of how a climate of institutional violence breeds further violent behavior. Dom Helder Camara, Archbishop of Recife in Brazil, calls it the spiral of violence.[5]

SPIRAL OF VIOLENCE

Violence #1
(Institutional Violence)

Poverty, Hunger, Racism, Sexism, Economic Exploitation.
  The injustices caused by institutional policies. After one complete cycle, also a direct result of Violence *#3*.

Violence #3
(Repression)

Suppression of Civil Rights, Dictatorships, Torture. . . .
  The powerful seek to reestablish "order."

Violence #2
(Counterviolence)

The Violence of Protest, Violent Resistance or Revolution, Armed Demonstrations, Terrorism, Sabotage.
  A struggle for more just conditions.
  Violence sometimes supported by both politics and religion.

Camara explains that the spiral begins with Violence #1, Institutional Violence, the violence in the rules or policies of institutions or systems that drive countless human beings into a subhuman condition, where they have to submit to humiliations and injustice, without hope. Their condition is that of slaves. Then the spiral proceeds to Violence #2: counterviolence. That is the violence that reacts to Violence #1—riots, revolutions, terrorism, and much of the crime we see in our own country today. Violence #3 is repression in response to Violence #2: it takes the form of bigger and better police and military forces.

Now, of course, a ten-year-old child is not going to be able to comprehend all the ramifications of this kind of analysis, but children can begin this understanding. They know they feel very frustrated in a situation in which they experience repression, whether it is in school or at home or in some kind of organization. They could tell us, and often do, that they "feel like hitting somebody."

And many children have first-hand experience of dictatorships. They often know what it means experientially to have someone else control your life, to be given no room to grow or to make decisions. They can begin to understand why someone or some group might strike out, even if the method seems counterproductive. That is a beginning in understanding the effects of institutional violence.

Dealing with a War Mentality in Our Culture

> I am tired of fighting. Our chiefs are killed. . . . It is cold and we have no blankets. The little children are freezing to death. My people, some of them have run away to the hills and have no blankets, no food; no one knows where they are—perhaps freezing to death. I want to have time to look for my children and see how many I can find. Maybe I shall find them among the dead. Hear me, my chiefs. I am tired; my heart is sick and sad. From where the sun now stands, I will fight no more forever [October 5, 1877—Chief Joseph of the Nez Percé Nation].[6]

It has been over a hundred years since Chief Joseph uttered these now well-known words of surrender. Chief Joseph knew the terrible cost of war: he pledged to "fight no more forever." We may question whether we today realize the cost of war. Modern warfare has raised the stakes in terms of the numbers of people affected, but the basic truth is that war means death.

In an introduction to one of the chapters in a study called *Children and War: Political Socialization to International Conflict,* author Howard Tolley quotes a child:

> I hate war because it kills and wounds. It takes our tax money and buys weapons with tax money. We could have built buildings with tax money to make an apartment house. Even kids in Vietnam [are being killed]. Why some kids are even 9 years old and that's why I HATE WAR.[7]

The question for us as parents is, what kind of attitudes are our children developing toward war? Are we and they mesmerized by the "war mentality" that is part of our culture? That mentality supports military resolutions to conflicts; states that our security as a nation rests on arms; and asserts that the United States is in military competition with other nations, especially the Soviet Union, so that the United States must be "Number One" in military strength. This war mentality argues that in the face of limited resources we have to be sure we keep what we have and preserve our access to future resources. Moreover, it states that to be a loyal American means to support the government no matter what its decisions about foreign policy and national defense. This mentality also manifests itself in relying on better armed police, tougher prisons, and capital punishment as the solution to crime—thus relying on the very institutional violence that often leads to crime.

One of the conclusions of Tolley's study about children's attitudes toward war is that parental influence is crucial. "Children's perspectives on war in general, their attitudes toward the Vietnam conflict, and knowledge about that war all share a close relationship to opinions reportedly heard from parents."[8]

What, then, are *our* attitudes about war? How aware are we of different manifestations of the war mentality in our everyday life? What kind of environment are we shaping for our children with regard to this mentality?

One area to look at is toys and other play situations. This statement from the Association for Childhood Education International is pointed: "To the war games which children have played in all times and in most cultures, have been added toys that explode, dolls that bleed, death rays that topple, tanks or ambulances that roar to the kill."[9]

The position that we have always taken with our children is that we do not think it is fun to pretend to kill people. We have told them that for that reason we will not buy them toy guns or rifles or tanks. However, this has not been an ironclad rule in our home. When Tommy was six he had several experiences with other children that indicated he was being intimidated by their use of toy guns. He said to Jim, "Dad, I *have* to have a gun. I have to defend myself." Jim attempted to suggest a solution that would meet his needs of self-defense but would not involve getting a gun. He said, "What if I make a bullet-proof shield for you? Then you'll be protected." Tommy stated emphatically, "That won't work. I have to have a gun!" Then he had a thought, and offered his own compromise, "How about a squirt gun? That just shoots water. It doesn't even shoot *pretend* bullets." We were struck by his ability to honor our values, yet come up with a way to meet his own needs. He got his squirt gun, and soon afterwards gun-playing ceased to be an issue in the neighborhood.

Several times we have allowed the children to have toys which have to do with weapons or fighting, like an outer-space battleship. We are not sure we should. But we do want to avoid creating an obsession about battle toys. Some things become "forbidden fruit" to a child, and take on much more importance than they would otherwise. Generally, we feel that the most important and long-lasting action we can take as parents is simply to let our children know how we feel about guns and war toys, and why we prefer other kinds of toys.

Television violence

Television is another part of our children's lives that has an indisputable effect on their attitudes toward violence and war. Much has been written and said about the effect of TV violence on children. While not all findings are absolutely conclusive, it is evident even to TV executives that TV violence has some negative effect on children. As far back as 1972, Elton H. Rule, an ABC official, said: "Now that we are reasonably certain that televised violence can increase aggressive tendencies in some children, we will have to manage our program planning accordingly."[10]

And yet the networks' own curtailing of violent shows over the past ten years has been minimal. Children still see a steady parade of aggressive behavior and violent resolution of conflict. The "good guys" are no different from the "bad guys" on this point. "Even the most casual of viewers can see that good guys use violence just as often as bad guys. Good guys, especially policemen and private detectives, are also likely to use illegal or somewhat shady tactics, such as breaking and entering without a search warrant. In the end all is justified, however, because the 'good guys' are on the side of truth and right."[11]

As we mentioned in Chapter 1, we try to limit the amount of TV our children watch, as well as censor to some extent *what* they watch. That censoring rules out most shows that include violence. However, we do watch some of those shows with them. We attempt to explain and answer questions about the behavior portrayed, as well as suggest other ways the characters might have been able to handle the conflict.

The pervasiveness in TV of violent behavior, especially by the upholders of truth and law, has a carry-over into attitude formation about the rightness of war. If children are being conditioned by TV to accept violent behavior, they will be less likely to question war. Studies show that fictionalized TV violence may even have more influence on children's war attitudes than newscasts showing actual combat episodes.

Children are also conditioned or influenced toward "pro-violence/war" attitudes by comic books, and even by other types of children's books. Comic book heroes very seldom use nonviolent methods to resolve conflicts. They support the belief that the true man (or woman, but usually the hero is a man) is a fighter, a modern-day warrior. Our own children read very few comics in our home but we are sure they read more when they are with other children. It seems essential, as with other kinds of reading, to talk with our children about what they read and how they feel about what they have read.

The concept of the "modern-day warrior" brings us to a consideration of the image of the military. It might be helpful, even with young children, to find out what their perceptions of the military are. What are soldiers? What do they do? Why do some people want to be soldiers? Why do some people not want to be soldiers? Such questions will of course eventually bring the family to a consideration of the realities of war itself, and we will discuss this below; but it is helpful in itself to get an idea of how our children feel about "being a soldier."

Older children, of course, have a more immediate reason to think about the military. As parents we need to be aware of military recruitment programs that are carried on in high schools. If there is a military recruitment campaign in a school, does the school provide opportunities for the students to hear the other side of the issue? JROTC programs are another concern. We think they need to be examined in terms of what kind of statement a school is making by sanctioning a JROTC program. Is the school saying it supports military resolutions of conflict to the point that it feels it is important for adolescents to begin training to be part of these resolutions? The leadership training and the discipline structure may be viewed favorably by some, but we would have questions about the overall influence on children of a school supporting a JROTC program.

Any discussion about attitudes toward war must include the question of the arms race. An action by Bishop Francis Reh of Saginaw, Michigan, speaks dramatically about our responsibility for children's attitudes toward war and weaponry. He forbade the Catholic schools and school children in his diocese to participate in a contest sponsored by the Navy to design a new emblem for the Trident submarine *U.S.S. Michigan*. The Trident, according to one of its former missile designers, Robert Aldridge, "can destroy 408 cities or military emplacements with a nuclear blast five times that which ripped into Hiroshima and Nagasaki."

According to *Sojourners* magazine, "in a letter of protest, Bishop Reh called the Trident contest a 'subtle indoctrination of children into a world of self-destructive weaponry,' and said he was offended that the Trident—'a horrifying instrument of unbelievable destructive power to life and earth'— was to be named after the state."[12]

The "subtle indoctrination" that the bishop notes is something we feel it is important to counter. Chapter 6 on social action mentions several kinds of activities in which our children have been involved as a way of protesting the madness of the nuclear race. Ann Mische, the fourteen-year-old daughter of outstanding peace educators Jerry and Pat Mische, was invited in the name of all children of the world to speak at an anti-nuclear prayer service in Washington, D.C., in November 1979. These are her words:

> My name is Ann Mische. I am speaking for children all over the world who are nuclear victims as much as anyone else. If nuclear energy and the production of nuclear weapons continue, we could grow up to find that the world which we have to live in has been poisoned by nuclear radiation, or destroyed by nuclear warfare. The decisions being made today in Washington and all over the world are decisions which we have no part in making, yet they could ruin the world for children in generations to come. It's our world, too, and we want to live![13]

Howard Tolley summarizes his findings in his study on children's attitudes toward war as follows: "In sum, children regard war in the abstract as immoral, yet they express important qualifications to commitments based on principle. The majority acknowledges a duty to fight for national defense, and a smaller proportion justify conflict against communists. Since the young appear willing to fight in wartime, their forecast of more conflict ahead may be read as either a self-fulfilling prophecy or a realistic appraisal of world affairs."[14]

"Indeed," writes Father Daniel Berrigan in an article in *New Catholic World,* "the children understand their plight more lucidly than we do— especially the children of that nation on which we visited the atomic firestorm. In a survey taken in Japan, fifth and sixth graders were asked: 'Do you think humanity will perish in your lifetime?' Their answer was overwhelmingly: 'Yes.' "[15]

All children, not just those in countries that have been devastated by war, are forming attitudes about war. It is our responsibility as parents to help them make their way through all they hear, read, and see, as well as so much they do not know. The authors of *Family Adventures Toward Shalom* say, "Many families deal with the problem of war by ignoring it or avoiding any discussion of it. When we do this, we subtly communicate a message that problems of international relations, war and peace are for *Experts Only*."[16] In their manual of family activities they have several suggestions about ways to encourage discussions of war-related issues. One is to watch a war movie together and then "debrief" it as a family. Old movies on TV might serve this purpose as well as current films.

Another idea is to put together a Peace Chronicle—a scrapbook of terrorist, war-type events from the news, rewritten with a peaceful headline, a peaceful solution. But besides such activities, it is our responsibility also to give our children straight factual information about war/peace issues.

Patriotism = willingness to fight?

Tommy has recently read *Sadako and the Thousand Paper Cranes* by Eleanor Coerr. It is the story of a Japanese girl who was two years old when the bomb fell on Hiroshima. As a result of the radiation exposure she developed leukemia and died when she was eleven. She was trying to get a thousand paper cranes made before she died. In her memory and as a call for peace today, often at memorial observances or peace demonstrations paper cranes are in evidence. Just talking to Tommy about the book has been a good way of opening up a discussion of the reality of war.

Sadako's story is not a pretty piece of reality for a child, but it is a face of war that a child should look at. Parents might want to make use of one or more films that are often available through a public library's film service. Some of these films would be excellent food for parent-child discussion groups. The *War. Peace. Film Guide* (Chicago: World Without War Publications) by Lucy Dougall is a good source for war/peace films.

The concept of nationalism or patriotism is one that bears mentioning here. What do we convey to our children about what it means to love one's country? Tolley's study contains this summary of children's thinking:

> A sixth grade girl best described the attitudes of most of the children surveyed when she wrote: "War is horrible, but we have to learn to live with it." In general, young people firmly believe war is wrong, *but* they feel at times it is needed. A quotation from another sixth grader illustrates the ambivalence which characterizes so many responses. "I don't think war is good, and I don't think we should have it. I guess it's ok if it's over a good cause and doesn't last very long." What do children feel is a "good cause" for war? Some in this survey believe that war is good "if the U.S. beats the communists." Far more, however, regard defense of the nation's freedom as the primary objective. One boy explained that conviction as follows: "We have to go to war for a purpose, to have a free country. . . . Every country has got to go to war sometime or another to defend themselves."[17]

Can a person be a patriot and still refuse to fight? We would say definitely yes. We would say that true patriotism is devotion to the *ideals* of one's country. That devotion can be transferred to the *policy* of one's country only when that policy is consistent with the ideals.

So our children need to see service to one's country as something broader than military service. They also need to understand why some people choose not to fight, what it means to be a conscientious objector. Certainly, if there is the opportunity to talk with someone who was or is a conscientious objector, that kind of discussion would be an invaluable aid. In our own family, Jim's explanation to the children of why he became a conscientious objector while he was in the National Guard has been enriching for all of us. We have overheard the children explaining to other people why their Daddy would not carry a gun.

Building an Interdependence Mentality

It is not enough simply to deal with the war mentality, the "us against them" way of thinking. We must at the same time be building a countermentality—a way of looking at the world as one family, an interdependent unit. For children of all ages, we feel there are several themes that are part of the bigger concept of interdependence: becoming comfortable with differences; developing a sense of oneness; understanding the systems or structures that influence people; and developing a sense of responsibility for strengthening ties among people.

Becoming comfortable with differences

This concept is handled extensively in the next chapter on multiculturalizing family life. Here we would only like to offer a few reflections on interna-

Tommy and Iran (or it isn't always easy!)

Within a couple of months of Iran's taking the 50 US hostages, Tommy informed us that he thought President Carter should send the Shah back to Iran, as the letter below indicates (we did not know until weeks afterwards that Tommy had send the letter to the President). Had we broken through the "us against them" mentality that was sweeping the country? We thought so, at least for a while. Then suddenly his attitude changed. By May 1980, six months after the hostages were taken, he wanted to buy the worst anti-Iran buttons around. So much for thinking the task is easy!

Dear Mr. Carter,

Please send the shah back to Iran and don't declare war just because your Congress wants to.

P. S. I don't want 50 people killed from our country because the shah is one person and the Iranians will kill the shah if we send him over. But if we don't send him over they'll kill 50 Americans and 50 is more than one so if they kill one person it will save 50 people.

pronounciation

McGinnis

A 9 year old boy,
named Tommy
McGinnis

tional differences. The TV show *Sesame Street* does a good job of helping children deal with Spanish-English language differences. They are presented to children as a normal part of living with other people. ("I say it this way. You say it this other way.") For young children, learning simple words and phrases for "good morning" "good-bye," "my name is," and the like in several languages can help to minimize fears and to develop feelings of respect for other languages and hence other people. As preschoolers our children enjoyed two books by Muriel Feelings, *Jambo Means Hello* and *Moja Means One.* The books are Swahili alphabet and counting books, wonderfully illustrated. Folkway Records has a series by Ella Jenkins that also does a good job of introducing young children to language differences.

Theresa has commented more than once on another person's speaking English with a foreign accent. When we explained to her that that person could speak two languages and had talked for a longer period of time in the other language, she saw the bilingual ability as something desirable.

Having pictures of people in various kinds of dress in our homes, whether it is by way of UNICEF calendars or posters, art work, or place mats affords the constant opportunity to talk about people of different lands.

Developing a sense of oneness

Simply having a globe or a world map in the home can provide opportunities for discussion of news items, as well as conversations about people from other countries. We feel that children can begin to understand the United Nations at an early age, too. When Theresa was in pre-school her class celebrated UN Day by talking about the purpose of the United Nations Organization and by reciting the World Pledge:[18]

> I pledge allegiance to the World
> To cherish every living thing,
> To care for earth and sea and air,
> With peace and freedom everywhere!

Families can also certainly celebrate UN Day. Music, pictures, foods from various lands, can be part of a party atmosphere. The whole concept of celebrating interdependently is an important one for all of us, especially for children. Chapter 1 on stewardship/simplicity recommended buying gifts from Third World outlets or other self-help groups. Exposing our children to days of celebration in other cultures is a way of helping them grow in knowledge about that culture while enjoying the experience. (For example, Kwanza is an African gift-giving festival. The "lessons of Kwanza" could provide much "food for fun" for children. (*Ebony, Jr.* in the December 1975 issue has a good explanation of Kwanza.)

When Jim and I were children we had pen pals. And that's still a good way of reaching to another culture. Of course, for most U.S. citizens that means the pen pal must read and write English. That fact alone can be a learning experience for our children. "Why are most U.S. citizens language-poor?"

Our own reading as well as our children's can reflect a commitment to learning about other people. For example, as adults and older children, the more we read newsletters like the ones put out by the Friends Committee on National Legislation and Bread for the World, the more we will understand the political and economic realities of our interdependence.

One way to help children understand factual global interdependence is to ask them to look at "My Global Day."

1. Where do the foods we eat come from?

2. Where do the raw materials used in making our clothes come from?

3. What about the materials for our cars? Appliances? Toys? Artifacts in our home?

Older children could draw lines from the family's home to places around the world on a large map to visualize the connectedness. A more elaborate version of this exercise is described in *Family Activities Toward Shalom*.[19]

Understanding systems and developing a sense of responsibility for action

Explaining the economic and political systems that come to bear on the production and distribution of food is a good way to help children understand systems and how they relate to global interdependence. Basically, we think it is important for children to understand and believe that *all* people have a right to food, not just those who have the money to buy it. And even young children can begin to understand that the way things are now, some people (especially people in the U.S.) have a lot more food than others. People in the U.S. eat high on the food chain—meaning we eat a lot of meat which is produced by using other food products (grains). Lastly, older children can understand what "food self-reliance" means—that nations need to be free to feed themselves and develop their own agricultural resources.

Now, specifically, how does one implement all this as a family? We certainly do not plan lectures on world hunger for family nights. But there are things we can do. Looking at the way we eat in terms of how much meat we eat is one way. Our family is in the process of reinstituting occasional poverty meals (rice or beans or potatoes), after which we all talk about why some people are fortunate if they have *that* much to eat.

Friends of ours in California, Bob and Janet, are experimenting in their family with ways to reduce their consumption of "cash crops." This is the way they explain their action. "Cash crops are grown in Third World countries where labor and land are cheap. The best soil is acquired for growing them while the native population lacks sufficient acreage to grow their basic food. Cash cropping works in plantation fashion, where the field workers are paid only two to three dollars for a twelve-hour day. Coffee and sugar top the cash-crop list. Other items are coconuts, pineapple, and bananas, along with many spices and nuts. Boycotting cash crops is a first step toward ending feudal systems which widen the gap between rich and poor."[20] The suggestions on diet and gardening in Chapter 1 on stewardship/simplicity would also be part of "eating interdependently."

A family connecting with another family in another part of the world can be a way of better understanding people and systems. Jim and I were fortunate enough to be able to travel to India in 1972. We still keep in touch with Akumar Kumar, a Gandhian village worker, and his family. Through them we can begin to explain world agricultural realities to the children. Why is irrigation difficult? Where do people of India sell what they grow? How does the Indian government help or hinder their efforts?

In the same way, parishes or community groups can pair with sister parishes or groups of other nations. This is a symbolic expression of interdependence, as well as a way to encourage learning about the problems faced by other nations.

Recently we found ourselves attempting to explain some difficult political realities to our children. Jim had given me a beautiful wall-hanging for Christmas that was made by women in Chile who are trying to support themselves and their children. Their husbands have been killed or imprisoned as political dissidents by the Chilean military government. We explained this to the children and asked them if they wanted to give some of their money, for instance by giving up a snack, to help support these women and their children. After many questions about why the men were in prison, our children saw that their own little help would be a good thing. To them giving a dime is meaningful.

One other economic/political reality that our children have become involved in with us is the boycott of Nestlé products. We have overheard both David and Tommy explain to friends why they will not eat Nestlé candy bars. Nestlé promotes the sale of infant formula to Third World women who can ill afford it, and thereby contributes to malnutrition.[21] The children can understand this to a degree (although for a while Tommy thought the formula was in the candy bars and that was why we were not buying them). They are proud to wear buttons promoting the boycott.

One last point needs to be made about economic and political systems and our responsibility for action to foster interdependence. Mahatma Gandhi once said, "There is enough in the world for everyone's need, but not for everyone's greed." As parents we need to stand as a counter-witness to what is called "life-boat ethics." Life-boat ethics says that since there is not enough for everyone, better *we who have* get into the life-boat than all those *who have not*. A good way to counter this concept for children is with the fantasy of Spaceship Earth:[22]

Just for a moment imagine that you are a first-class passenger on a huge spaceship with thousands of passengers travelling through space at a speed of 66,000 mph. You discover that the craft's environment system is faulty. Passengers in some sections are actually dying due to the emission of poisonous gases into their oxygen supply. Furthermore, you learn that there is a serious shortage of provisions—food supplies are rapidly diminishing and the water supply, thought previously to be more than adequate, is rapidly becoming polluted due to fouling from breakdowns in the craft's waste and propulsion systems.

To complicate matters even more, in the economy sections where passengers are crowded together under the most difficult of situations, it is reported that many are seriously ill. The ship's medical officers are able to help only a fraction of the sick, and medicines are in short supply.

Mutinies have been reported, and although some of the crew and passengers are engaged in serious conflict in one of the compartments, it is hoped that this conflict is being contained successfully; however, there is widespread fear as to what may happen if it cannot be contained or resolved within that compartment.

The spacecraft has been designed with an overall destruct system, the controls of which have been carefully guarded. Unfortunately the number of technologists who have gained access to the destruct system has increased, and all of the crew and passengers have become uneasy due to evidences of mental instability in some of those gaining such access.

We could go on, but the point is: what would you do if put in such a position? Now that you have imagined this situation, you are ready to face reality. You are on such a spaceship right now—Spaceship Earth.[22]

Conclusion

In 1963 in the Encyclical *Peace on Earth*, Pope John XXIII wrote, "If this [peace] is to come about, the fundamental principle on which our present peace depends must be replaced by another, which declares that the true and solid peace of nations can consist, not in equality of arms, but in mutual trust alone."[23]

Many centuries before that, the prophet Isaiah wrote, "Then the wolf shall be the guest of the lamb, and the leopard shall lie down with the kid. The calf and the young lion shall browse together, with a little child to guide them" (Isaiah 11:6).

That little child is in our hands. It is our charge to help children develop the trust of which Pope John speaks, so that they can contribute to the day when the wolf and lamb will be able to lie together.

CHAPTER 4

MULTICULTURALIZING OUR FAMILY LIFE

Theresa was only a year old and Tommy was about five. I (Kathy) was talking to Tommy about Theresa's Native American heritage, about what it means to be a member of the Winnebago Nation. He listened patiently to my explanation. Then he looked up and asked "Mommy, when Theresa grows up will she kill us?"

We think back to that incident often. It was a startling indication to us of how deeply ingrained stereotypes, misconceptions, and fears can be, even at a very early age. Tommy, who at that time did not know any Indian people besides Theresa, had a very clear and very negative idea about what Indians do to people. We thought we had screened out sources of negative attitudes, but apparently we had not.

The question that was with us then still challenges us today: How can we create an environment in our family that encourages a sense of respect for people from a variety of races and cultures? How can we do this in a society that works to keep groups of people apart from each other and promotes the growth of false ideas and fears about "the other"?

When we talk about "multiculturalizing" our family life we have several basic goals in mind. Spelling out these goals is a way of defining "multi-culturalizing."

1. To build and strengthen a sense of self, a feeling of pride in one's own racial and cultural heritage.

2. To provide concrete examples of the common needs and values of all people, no matter what their skin color or nationality. To help children see that there are many ways in which all people are the same.

3. To encourage and actively promote a deep respect for racial and cultural differences and a capacity for rejoicing in and learning from, rather than merely tolerating, these differences. In 1 Corinthians 12 Saint Paul uses the analogy of the body, calling to mind that the body is made up of *different* parts, all essential to its functioning. "If all the parts were the same, how could it be a body?" he asks. All children should have the opportunity to experience the beauty and the richness of different cultures.

4. To develop an awareness of the world as one human family, with people struggling and working together, and eventually living more fully as interde-

pendent beings, as builders of the Kingdom. To provide concrete examples and suggestions about how this "world family" sense of interdependence can be fostered.

5. To become more aware of how racial and cultural differences have been and are being unjustly handled in our society; in other words, to understand what racism is, how it works, and what can be done to fulfill the charge of Isaiah, "to loose the fetters of injustice, to untie the knots of the yoke, to let the oppressed go free, and to release those who have been crushed" (Isa. 61:1–2).

Rationale for Multiculturalizing Family Life

The society in which we live is plagued by many problems. The mission of Christ is "to restore all things to God," as Paul says. We are Christ's agents. We are to bring Christ to the society in which we live. In order to do this, in order to be *effective* workers in the vineyard, we need to understand these problems as completely as we can.

Racial prejudice, discrimination, and the oppressive dynamic of racism itself are forces that have torn at the foundation of the Kingdom for centuries. The prayer of Jesus "that we all may be one" is not realized when society thus continues to divide itself. Some of society's divisions are created and maintained by racist policies and practices in institutions that shape our attitudes and our behavior. As parents we must stand against these policies and practices, and take definite steps to change them. This action for change is part of what it means to multiculturalize our family life and to work to multiculturalize our society.

Our charge to do this comes directly from Scripture. The U.S. Catholic Bishops in *Brothers and Sisters to Us: Pastoral Letter on Racism in Our Day* express it this way:

> The Christian response to the challenges of our times is to be found in the Good News of Jesus. The words that signaled the start of His public ministry must be the watchword for every Christian response to injustice. "He unrolled the scroll and found the passage where it was written: The spirit of the Lord is upon me; therefore, he has anointed me. He has sent me to bring glad tidings to the poor, to proclaim liberty to captives, recovery of sight to the blind and release to prisoners, to announce a year of favor from the Lord. Rolling up the scroll he gave it back . . . and sat down. . . . 'Today this Scripture passage is fulfilled in your hearing.' "
>
> God's word proclaims the oneness of the human family—from the first words of Genesis, to the "Come, Lord Jesus" of the Book of Revelation. God's word in Genesis announces that all men and women are created in God's image; not just some races and racial types, but all bear the imprint of the Creator and are enlivened by the breath of His one Spirit.[1]

The Society of Friends, or Quakers, challenge themselves corporately and individually to work directly in society to make that vision from Scripture a reality.

> Enunciation of the principle of equality among human beings in the sight of God is important and necessary, but it is not sufficient. Realization of equality involves such matters as independence and control of one's own life. Therefore, friends must aid the efforts of the exploited to attain self-determination and social, political and economic justice, even when their attainment involves changes in attitudes and practices formerly taken for granted.
>
> The goal of good human relations is a community in which each individual and each group can feel sure of opportunities for self-development, full realization of potential, and rewarding relations with others.[2]

In addition to the Scriptural/religious motivation for multiculturalizing our family, there are basic psychological/sociological reasons for it. Children from every racial group need to feel good about their own racial identity. They also need to know that their racial identity does not make them better or worse than any other racial group.

Minority children in our culture (Blacks, Asian-Americans, Native Americans, and Hispanics) constantly receive messages from society telling them that they are inferior. Their own psychological well-being demands that at home they receive a real foundation of pride in being Black, Puerto Rican, Chinese, and so on. Consider this statement from members of the United Parents of East San Diego:

> CHICANO CHILDREN: IMMUNIZE THEM EARLY. In this country minority children are taught that they are of little value. Therefore the pressing problem for Chicano parents is to develop their children's pride in identifying with their own people. . . .
>
> It is crucial to provide our children with constant reassurance, so that when they are assaulted by white society—as they will be—they understand that the fault is not their own. . . .
>
> We must develop our children's skills for critical analysis. The books they read, the TV programs they watch, their school assignments all give out messages which can be harmful. We must take the time to talk with our children and help them learn to analyze these messages and immunize them against racism, sexism and class injustice. And we must help them to become educated, not for the goal of individual "success," but in order to be better prepared to struggle for their people.[3]

What Chicano parents say could be said by any minority parents.

The situation is different for white children in our culture. White children constantly receive messages from the culture that say to be white is to be somehow superior to people of color. Abraham Citron in his study *The "Rightness" of "Whiteness"* says that this kind of "white-centric" world is damaging to white children themselves. White children come naturally to accept white as a norm or standard and to see other skin colors as deviations from the norm, and therefore deviations from real people.[4] For example, to be a "baby" for many white children would mean to look like the babies on the Pampers boxes or the baby food jars; "baby" means "white baby." This situation gives white children a false sense of self and hampers them in functioning harmoniously with people of different races.

Multiculturalizing our families and society is part of creating a peace-filled world for our children. It is a way of helping them develop the skills to be agents of that peace. A truly multicultural way of thinking would counteract concepts of cultural superiority (ethnocentrism) among the general American population, who would then refuse to elect political leaders or sanction public policies that reflected a concept of cultural superiority. Ways of implementing ethnocentric concepts often follow a path of subtle progression. If we are superior, then they are inferior. If they are inferior, then one of two attitudes often follows. First, they need our help because they can't help themselves—through no fault of their own, of course. Thus, it becomes our "manifest destiny" or our "white man's burden" to provide our answers to their problems. Or, secondly, a much more overtly destructive attitude develops. One of its crassest expressions came from the Vietnam War: "Those Orientals have little regard for human life." The actions that followed from that attitude, such as the My Lai massacre, were almost beyond belief. Further development of war/foreign policy questions can be found in Chapter 3.

Looking at Ourselves

But how do we do it? Actually and concretely, how do you multiculturalize a family?

We would suggest that the place to begin is with ourselves—our own attitudes, our behavior, the things we do around the house, and the choices we make about the kind of environment we live in.

Taking a look at our own attitudes about anything can be difficult. Taking a look at our own attitudes about race can be frightening. There are times when we do not like what we see in ourselves, times when we have to admit we are not comfortable with our fears, questions, resentments, uneasiness. We are certain we would like to feel and think differently. And often we know with even greater certainty that we would like our children to think and feel differently than we do.

There is no magic formula for changing racial attitudes. Help comes in different forms, at different times, and from different sources. Jim and I have often thought back on incidents in our lives that have been and continue to be significant in the reshaping of our own racial attitudes: living in Memphis at the time of the assassination of Dr. Martin Luther King; a racial awareness workshop in our parish in the early 1970s; reading *The Autobiography of Malcolm X;* a trip to India in 1972; reading two books by Lois Stalvey—*The Education of a Wasp* and *Getting Ready;* moving to an integrated neighborhood; and especially, gentle prodding by Black and Native American friends.

We would like to suggest here three of the exercises that we and others have found helpful in evaluating our own racial attitudes/background.

1. Examining our own prejudices

—List just for yourself or in a group session with others three attitudes or beliefs of yours that you consider to be examples of racial prejudice.

Example: "Blacks are intellectually inferior to whites."

—List three ways in which you could change or challenge those attitudes.

Example: See and listen to intellectual and highly trained Blacks.

—List one thing you could do to put yourself in a situation that might help to bring about that change.

Example: Enroll in a course taught in a Black institution.

2. Looking back on significant experiences

—During a time for reflection write down one incident in your life that changed your attitude toward a certain group of people. Note what your thinking was before that incident, and what it was afterwards.

—Is there any way that kind of incident can now be duplicated for yourself? For your children?

Example: You once thought Puerto Rican youths were interested solely in gang wars and stealing. Then you worked for a short time with a social agency's program in a Puerto Rican neighborhood. You saw Puerto Rican people very concerned with family, education, church activities, and so on.

3. Taking another look at our past: Racial profile

These questions refer to your own racial experiences and background. You may want to use them as a basis for group discussion. Give particular attention to Question 8.

1. What is the racial composition of the people with whom you work?

2. What is the racial composition of the neighborhood in which you live?

3. Have you attended any racial awareness workshops or training sessions in the past three years? If yes, briefly describe these sessions.

4. What has been the racial character of your educational experiences? (Racial identity of fellow students, teachers, etc.)

5. Have any previous living or working experiences put you in contact with

a significant number of minority people? (If there are many of these experiences, list just the most recent three.)

6. What notable Black person do you admire the most: *(a)* in your own area/city; *(b)* on a national scale.

7. Answer Question 6 in terms of *(a)* Hispanic (local, national), *(b)* Native American (local, national), *(c)* Asian (local, national).

8. Using the scale below, how would you assess your racial experience/background?

Totally your   Totally
own race   multi-racial

1   2   3   4   5   6   7   8   9

Where would you like to be on that scale five years from now?
What one thing can you best do now to move yourself toward that point?

Another way of looking at ourselves is simply to look at our home environment.

4. Visuals in the home

Children pick up some unstated messages about people from the visual representations they see in our homes. We feel it is important to have pictures around our home of people of all races. The same, we feel, applies to religious art; we have an African madonna in our living room, and our "Jesus and Children" picture shows children of many races. John and Sylvia, a Black couple, have their home filled with pictures of Black people. They feel that their three sons are strengthened in their own sense of self by seeing these images in their home. They also feel that their sons are not going to get that visual reinforcement in school, so it becomes doubly important for them to experience it in their home.

5. Reading materials in the home

Recently Theresa and I read a biography of Fannie Lou Hamer, the Black civil rights activist. The book talked about Ms. Hamer's dedication to working for the rights of Black people. We think models such as Fannie Lou Hamer are important for Theresa, who is Native American and Black, in terms of self-image. But they are important for children of any racial group; stories of these people are occasions for discussion about how racism got started and why people are still struggling against it today. In addition to biographies, the kinds of books and magazines that are in the home have a lot to do with attitude formation in children. Our children enjoy looking at the pictures in

Ebony, Jr. (a Black-oriented children's magazine, 820 S. Michigan Ave., Chicago, IL 60605), and our nine-year-old enjoys reading it. Our children have commented on pictures in *Ebony* itself. ("That's a pretty lady. She has hair like Mrs. Brown.") Reading is, of course, an excellent source of knowledge-gathering, both for ourselves and our children.

Besides the *Ebony* periodicals (we prefer *Ebony, Jr.* to *Ebony*), we would recommend for adults:

Black Scholar (P.O. Box 908, Sausalito, CA 94965) contains heavily researched analyses of current social, political, and educational trends from a Black perspective.

Akwesasne Notes (Mohawk Nation, via Rooseveltown, NY 13683) presents news about Native peoples of North and South America. It includes a poetry section and an extensive list of resources (such as a beautiful calendar). It is highly political.

Nuestro (P.O. Box 4255, El Paso, TX 79914) is a Hispanic publication modeled on *Time* and *People* magazines.

Ebony, Jr. is a good resource for children's books. But the best single resource we have found is the *Bulletin* of the Council on Interracial Books for Children (1841 Broadway, New York, NY 10023), featuring quite a complete review section of books for children of all ages. Through the recommendations of the Council we have started building a "multicultural library" for our children, as well as becoming much more selective about our use of the public library.

6. Friends in our home

What about the people who come into our homes, the people our children call our friends? If the situations in our lives from which friendships usually spring are all white (church, work, neighborhood, civic activities, social activities), then it is going to be hard to make friends of people of other races. We have found that the more we have broadened our range of contacts—integrated neighborhood and school, attendance at local American Indian Pow Wow, and so on—the more multicultural our friendships have become. It is hard to encourage our children to have friends from different racial groups if they see us only with friends of our own race and culture.

7. Outside enrichment

Margaret, one of our friends, took her thirteen- and six-year-old sons to hear Chief Fools Crow of the Oglala Sioux Nation at a local university. She said her children talked about the experience for long after. She had the same results when her children heard Alex Haley.

Films, theatre, and art exhibits, too, are good ways to broaden our perspectives. We have spent periods of time with our children in the Native American section of the Westward Expansion museum in Saint Louis. We are trying to help them appreciate Native American cultures as well as begin to understand that to Native American people "Westward Expansion" meant devastation.

8. Professional services

If our children encounter minority adults only in serving capacities (as janitors, maids, waiters, etc.) it becomes more difficult to counter the stereotype that minority people are not as capable as whites. Children need role models of "important people" from a variety of racial groups. Our children's dentist is Black. Twice, when they had to go to medical specialists, we asked our pediatrician to recommend a Black.

9. Toys

An analysis of children's toys is an important learning opportunity for us and our children alike. How many of their toys (puzzles, picture books, dolls, games) give them anything but white images? And a special note of warning on toys, books, and television programs that deal with "Indians": it is essential to counter the prevalent stereotype of Native Americans as war-loving savages. Packages of little plastic cowboys and Indians always have the Indians with rifles or tomahawks.

We have found some Black dolls, a few puzzles with Black images, and friends of ours have a Black history game. A toy company called Shindana Toys (6107 S. Central, Los Angeles, CA 90001) promotes "ethnically accurate" toys. For the most part, however, the choices are meager.

10. Our neighborhood, church, school, social community

Some questions to think about: Do we live in an integrated neighborhood? Do our children attend an integrated school? Are the "authority" figures in our children's school racially mixed? Jim and I are fortunate in having had Asian, Black, and White teachers for our children. We have occasionally suggested to teachers that resource people from still other racial and cultural groups be brought in, so that the children see that knowledge comes from people from all races.

In some parts of the United States, multiracial neighborhoods, schools, churches, and so on, are easy to come by. In other areas it is possible to live at least in a bi-racial neighborhood. However, there are still many neighborhoods that are "one-race" areas. Obviously, the ideal situation for children in terms of their attitude formation is to have opportunities to play with children from many different racial and cultural groups on an everyday basis. We moved into an integrated neighborhood for that reason. But that is not possible for many people for many reasons. If your neighborhood is all one race we hope our other suggestions about our immediate environment will help fill that void.

11. Other family members

In the attempt to create a multicultural environment for our children, the attitudes and behavior of family members is crucial. A story from friends, Tom and Marie, is illustrative. "For Susie's second birthday we bought her a Black doll, so she wouldn't have only white ones. Susie loves the doll and treats it as she treats all the others. Well, one morning she carried the Black doll over to Marie's dad and put it on his lap. He was uncomfortable. He made three separate comments with racial overtones—"That doll has a sun-tan . . . Little Black Sambo . . . colored." At two Susie was too young for the comments to mean anything—we hope. But should we say anything to Marie's dad?"

In one sense the question is unanswerable. But from another point of view it needs to be addressed. Relatives and friends must know where we stand and what we are attempting to build for our children. They should be discouraged from saying or doing things that counteract what we are trying to do with our children; sometimes we can say something like, "I'm uncomfortable when you. . . ." On the other hand, our relationships are very important, and people need to be accepted where they are even as we all struggle to change.

Looking at the Culture

What are the prevalent messages about people of various racial/cultural groups that come to us through different cultural media—TV, movies, books, curricular materials in schools, and so on? We believe that the overwhelming one is that the white western cultures are superior to all others. We do think that some white western cultures (e.g., Eastern European) have *not* on the whole been handled adequately by the media and the schools; however, we feel that the prevailing attitude is that the white western world is the center of all that is industrious, cultural, and important.

This message comes in various forms. Our first concern is to identify the stereotypes that are manifestations of this message. "Africans are canni-bals." "Blacks are lazy." "Chinese have slits for eyes." "Indians wear feathers."

Parents have been dealing with these familiar statements for many years. These statements uttered by both children and adults are examples of ste-reotypic thinking. A racial-cultural stereotype can be defined as "an untruth or oversimplification about the traits and behaviors common to an entire race or cultural group."[5] Stereotypes, by their nature, tend to screen out per-ceptions which run counter to the oversimplification. We feel it is important to specify these stereotypes for our children because that makes it easier to identify them on TV, in books, movies, jokes, and so on. The appendix below lists common stereotypes of racial groups. Each list is divided into two categories: stereotypes young children may have already acquired, and stereotypes generally formulated at a later age. Parents can use the list both to check their own attitudes and to guide them in their work with their children.

Racial/cultural stereotypes come from various sources. There is sometimes a *grain* of truth in them; but they purport to reflect a whole truth about a whole group of people, which they do not. For example, some Chinese American people do work in laundries. This was truer in the past when they were excluded from other jobs. However, today Chinese Americans do many different kinds of jobs.

Stereotypes are perpetuated by cultural messengers—TV, books, comic strips, magazines, various forms of advertising, toys, decorations, costumes, jokes, amusement park motifs—as well as by "remarks" people make. Stereotypes are harmful in several ways.

—They promote misinformation about whole groups of people.

—They damage the self-images of whole groups of people.

—They are often used to justify keeping people in subordinate positions. In other words, they are used to bolster racism. For example, if we believe that Blacks have more brawn than brain, then we do not challenge the fact that Blacks are grossly underrepresented in managerial and professional positions.

As parents we must deal with racial stereotypes on several levels. First, there is the need to be aware of the prevalence of these stereotypes; we need to work continually to raise our own level of awareness as well as that of our children. The more skilled we become at spotting stereotypic portrayals of racial groups, the more we will be able to help our children spot these distortions.

Then comes the question of what to do about them. I had an enlightening experience with Theresa. As we were walking to school one morning she said to me, "Mommy, when are you going to tell Ms. Damos (her kindergarten teacher) to take down that picture that says 'I is for Indian' "? (Several weeks before, David's first-grade teacher had substituted "I is for Itch," which may have given Theresa the idea.) Feeling that my hand had been called, I did talk to Theresa's teacher, and she agreed to substitute "*I* is for Igloo" in her alphabet set.

I say, I felt my hand had been called. Theresa's remark had not come out of the blue. We had talked a little with the children about stereotypes (without using the word), especially about stereotyping of Indian people. As a family we had several times watched an excellent filmstrip produced by the Council on Interracial Books for Children called "Unlearning Indian Stereotypes." The children had become increasingly aware of things that have the effect of trivializing Indian dress or customs or otherwise "making fun of Indian people." There is a line in the filmstrip, which is narrated by Indian children, that says, "Books don't say '*I* is for Italian.' No! They say '*I* is for igloos, insects, inkwells and Indians.' Like Indians are *things,* instead of real people."[6] Theresa was responding to that concept when she asked me to ask the teacher to change that alphabet card.

There are other times when, even though no specific corrective action is taken, it is still important to point out the stereotype in order to keep awareness growing. When Tommy was eight he brought home a joke book from the school library. One of the jokes was demeaning to Chinese people, both in costuming and caption. Tommy pointed it out to me with, "You're not going to like this." So we talked about why I wouldn't like it. I think Tommy understood some of what I said. We did not change the book; but we understood each other a little better.

The more acutely we are aware of stereotypes, the more opportunities will present themselves to work for change. Books can present a variety of such opportunities. Children's books can be powerful allies in creating positive images of all kinds of people, or they can set up roadblocks along the way to those images. Books need to be evaluated for the racial images they present, just as for their values with respect to sexism (see Chapter 5). Here are some practical guidelines we would like to offer.[7]

1. Check the visuals

   a. How many of the pictures in this book are of minority people? Are non-Black minorities pictured?

   b. Are there pictures of minority people helping whites?

   c. Do any of the visuals reflect stereotypes listed in the appendix of this chapter?

2. Check the language

   a. Do the words themselves reinforce stereotypes? ("Savage hordes of Indians," "inscrutable Chinese")

   b. Do the characters' names reflect a variety of racial/cultural backgrounds? (Ms. Gonzalez, Mr. Ogura, Mr. Walkingstick, Ms. Kaminski)

3. Check the lifestyles portrayed

   a. Are the lifestyles of minorities portrayed very narrowly? (Blacks and Puerto Ricans living in poverty, Native Americans in trouble with alcoholism, Chicanos as migrant laborers)

   b. Are there lifestyles presented which could work as counterforces to stereotypes? (Black families with two parents, strong Asian women who are neither "China dolls" nor sexy "dragon ladies," African people who are advanced artistically and intellectually)

   c. Are the lifestyles and situations or minority people presented as inferior to those of whites?

4. Check the heroes and other role models

   a. Are minority people shown who have worked or are working for the rights of their racial group? (Paul Robeson, Cesar Chavez, Julius Nyerere, Patsy Mink, Mahatma Gandhi)

   b. Are minority men and women shown in positions of authority?

5. Look at the relationships between people

   a. Do the minority people function mainly in roles that put them in a position of inferiority to whites?

   b. Are people from different racial/cultural groups shown working together toward common goals?

6. Consider institutional racism

   a. Is there any indication in the book of the problems minorities face in this society?

   b. Does the story tend to "blame the victim"? In other words, does it leave the reader with the impression that victims of racism could get out from under oppressive situations if only they worked hard enough?

   c. Is there any indication that solutions to racism demand more than individual good will—that *structures* must change?

7. Check the author/editor

   a. How many of the books your children read have been written or edited by a member of a racial minority group?

   b. Are books or stories about a given group of people written by someone from that group?

Dealing with Racism in Institutions that Affect the Family

Racism is "any attitude, action or institutional structure which subordinates a person or group because of their color."[8] Institutional racism is such subordination occurring through the action or practice of some fairly stable social arrangement (schools, business, churches, etc.). Stokely Carmichael and Charles Hamilton explain institutional racism this way:

> When white terrorists bomb a Black church and kill five Black children, that is an act of individual racism, widely deplored by most segments of society. But when in that same city—Birmingham, Alabama—five hundred Black babies die each year because of the lack of proper food, clothing, shelter, and proper medical facilities, and thousands more are destroyed or maimed physically, emotionally, and intellectually because of conditions of poverty and discrimination in the Black community, that is a function of institutional racism.[9]

Racism always involves power. In fact, a very simple formula for racism is "Power + Prejudice = Racism" (from *Developing New Perspectives on Race,* by Pat A. Bidol[10]). A further development of this thought comes from Dr. Delmo Della-Dora, "Racism is different from racial prejudice, hatred, or discrimination. Racism involves having the power to carry out systematic discriminatory practices through the major institutions of our society."[11]

The institutional racism in institutions such as education, housing, employment, churches, media, and so on, can seem overwhelming. But it is not as if nothing can be done about it. It would be presumptuous and naive to imply that institutional racism is a simple phenomenon, and absurd to imply that it can be changed easily or quickly. On the other hand, it is crucial that we realize that as parents there are definite things we can do to effect changes. Parents have been successful in fighting racism in many institutions—housing, employment, the church, the legal system, and elsewhere.

Following are some guidelines on racism in education, the media, and other cultural institutions. They are not meant to be exhaustive; rather they are intended to be suggestive of the kinds of questions that need to be asked, as well as some examples of actions that parents have taken.

Schools

Racism occurs in education when:

—opportunities for minority children are inferior to those for white children

—decision-making power in the school system rests solely with whites

—positive role models from different racial groups are not presented in the school

—the curriculum presents only a white perspective

Some questions parents can ask:

1. What percentage of the professional staff is from minority groups?

2. What percentage of the school board or decision-making body is from minority groups?

3. Is the curriculum reviewed regularly to screen out racial distortions and to include positive images of all racial groups?

4. If there are minority children in the school, do they have the same facilities, privileges, opportunities as the white children?

5. Do the teachers have high academic and behavioral expectations for the minority children?

Three examples of actions:

Minnie, a Black mother in a large midwestern city, waged a court battle for years to desegregate the school system. The courts finally decided in her favor.

Roni, a white mother in a suburban school district, confronted the principal of her nine-year-old son's school about a racist remark her son had overheard a teacher make to a Black child. Thus the principal was made aware that both the child and the parent would watch teacher behavior in this area.

Josephine, a Black parent, backed her teenage son when he challenged his English teacher about an assigned novel that contained insulting references to Blacks. The novel was taken off the "required" list.

Media and other cultural institutions

Racism in the communications media and other institutions of the culture (amusement parks, toys, greeting cards, etc.) occurs when:

—reporting and programming of events that concern minority people are omitted;

—the reporting and programming concerning minority people is regularly done from a white perspective;

—stereotypic images of minority people are presented.

Some questions parents can ask:

1. What do TV shows tell us and our children about Blacks? Chicanos? Puerto Ricans? Chinese? Japanese? Native Americans? Africans? other Asians? . . . . (Fill in with other groups)

The following "Family TV Survey" worksheet might be helpful in answering this question.

FAMILY TV SURVEY

List the shows you watch, and then answer the following questions:

a. Who are the main characters? (Name them for each show.)
  How many of these are
  White?_____ Black?_____ Asian?_____ Hispanic?_____
  Native American?_____

b. Who are major supporting characters? (Again, name them.)
  How many are
  White?_____ Black?_____ Asian?_____ Hispanic?_____
  Native American?_____

c. Commercials—List the products for which you see commercials, and the number of times a product is advertised.
  Now count up the total number of commercials:_____
  Number of commercials with minority characters?_____
  (Make special note if any of these minority characters are of racial minorities other than Black.)

d. Newscasters:
  National news: Whites _____
                              Minorities_____
  Local news: Whites_____
                              Minorities_____
  Anchors on news shows: Whites_____
                              Minorities_____
  (Again, note if the minority newscasters are other than Black.)

e. How would you describe the Indian characters you see on TV shows or in TV movies? (Name the shows and movies.)

2. Have we ever expressed our concern to a TV or radio station, an amusement park, or the like, about the racial implications of their programs or

entertainment? A good example of the expression of such concern is the story of Leroy Zimmerman and his son Joel. They attended a Boy Scout Circus; this is an excerpt from Leroy's letter to the Chairperson of the Circus afterwards commenting on the "Indian Pageantry" act.

> In reflecting on the Indian Pageantry act, I wondered what need or purpose did the "playing Indian" serve. I was confused when there was an attempt by the narrator to give some background on Native Americans and the dancing exhibition only to be followed by the "Mr. Johnson and the Little Scouts" act depicting a scalping scene of "Mr. Johnson" by his befeathered undisciplined scout pack.
>
> Frankly, I was appalled by the blatant exhibit of a negative stereotype about American Indians in the name of humanitarian scouting. Even though the scalping scene was to be humorous, I feel the exhibition was a tragedy which made a negative impression on the young scouts that it is all right to believe that Native Americans scalp people.
>
> I do not appreciate having my son exposed to negative stereotyping of Native Americans or any other people within scouting activities.[12]

Another group of parents took action about another distorted image of Native Americans. Roni (White), Mary (White), Beulah (Cherokee), Amy (Rosebud Sioux), George (Mesquakie), and others, protested the theme of a ride at an amusement park on the grounds that it was a stereotypic portrayal of Native Americans and was offensive to them and their children. The ride has subsequently been "rethemed" and the offensiveness removed.

3. Do any of the places where we and our children go for entertainment reflect a stereotypic image of a certain group of people?

4. Do toys, greeting cards, and so on in our home reflect a stereotypic image of a certain group of people?

Children and parents together can check out toy stores to see what kinds of images of different racial groups the toys present. If there is not a multicultural selection they can ask the manager to make a change. Consumer pressure is still a powerful force.

Conclusion

In some ways the task of multiculturalizing our family environment is an overwhelming one. There are so many obstacles to doing what we want to do. But there are also rewards. When a relative says, "Since you've moved into an integrated neighborhood, I'm beginning to think that I was wrong about what happens to a neighborhood when Blacks move in," or when one's own child says, "I don't think we should watch this TV show because it's making fun of Indians," then we feel maybe something is making a difference.

Lois and Bill are friends of ours. They told us of an incident with their eighteen-year-old daughter that brought a different kind of reward. Helen was working on an assignment for an English Composition course. The assignment was to write a true autobiographical composition titled "Loss of Innocence." Helen wrote about an incident in which, some years before, her fifth-grade teacher had made racist comments in the class about a classmate, a child who happened to be very dark-skinned. Helen wrote that for her that experience meant a loss of innocence, in the sense that up to that time she had thought all adults believed and behaved the way her mother and father did toward people of other racial groups. Superficially, that experience could not have been a positive one for Helen; but it raised her consciousness of her parents' values as a countersign to other values in the culture. And she could write in her conclusion, "Now I can see more clearly what my Mom and Dad stand for, and why their values are important to me."

In the words of the U.S. Catholic Bishops, "We should influence the members of our families, especially our children, to be sensitive to the authentic human values and cultural contributions of each racial grouping in our country. . . . The difficulties of these new times demand a new vision and a renewed courage to transform our society and achieve justice for all" (from *Brothers and Sisters to Us: U.S. Bishops' Pastoral Letter on Racism in Our Day*).

APPENDIX ON COMMON RACIAL STEREOTYPES

Asians and Asian Americans

The term "Asian" rather than "Oriental" is used here since "Oriental" often carries a connotation of the exotic and mysterious.

Stereotypes commonly accepted by young children

—look alike
—have yellow skin and slits for eyes
—are very polite
—are always bowing
—celebrate exotic festivals, such as the Chinese New Year

Chinese Americans . . .
—favor dragons or dragon-like symbols as the essence of Chinese culture
—do not wear normal clothes
—necessarily have Fu Manchu mustaches
—speak a strange brand of English, filled with expressions like "Ah, so!" or "Number-one son"

Stereotypes commonly accepted by adults and older children

—live in quaint communities in the midst of large cities and cling to "outworn" alien customs
—are timid and soft-spoken, the model minority, excessively obedient, passive, docile, smiling, calm, peaceful
—yet, within, are sinister, sly, evil, cunning, cruel
—place little value on human life
—have succeeded by working hard and not rocking the boat
—are inscrutable
—are best suited for menial work, e.g., waiter, houseboy, cook, hand laundry (Chinese)
—are best suited for gardening and flower arranging (Japanese)

Africans

Stereotypes commonly accepted by young children

—are savage
—all live in huts and wear costumes or no clothes at all
—practice witchcraft and voodoo (witchdoctors, magic potions)
—live in or close to the jungle, with wild animals
—are cannibals
—have bones in their noses

Stereotypes commonly accepted by adults and older children

—are a primitive people
—have very little diversity of language, culture, history, or geography across the continent
—have no real religion
—are unable to master the English language
—observe very exotic customs
—sing and dance a lot
—are not capable of ruling themselves

Native Americans

The term "Native American" is used here because it is a self-definition. The word "Indian" is a European term for Native people. Currently the terms "Native American" and "American Indian" tend to be used interchangeably. We use the term "nation" instead of "tribe" because the latter carries a connotation of a primitive lifestyle.

Stereotypes commonly accepted by young children

—are savage and love to kill
—scalp white people
—have red skin

—all live in tipis
—speak in grunts and "ughs" and "hows" and "me-want-ems"
—all wear feathers

Stereotypes commonly accepted by adults and older children

—are primitive people
—are exotic and mystical
—look and act and live in the same way today as they did a hundred years or more ago
—have no authentic religion
—share the same lifestyle, culture, customs, across different nations as well as in different geographical settings (i.e., urban and reservation)
—are all supported by government handouts and not interested in working
—drink too much
—are noble children of nature
—are stoic

Hispanics

We use the term "Hispanic" in a generic sense to include people who are native to Latin American countries, as well as citizens of the U.S. who are of Latin American descent.

Stereotypes commonly accepted by young children

—are dirty, greasy people
—are brown-eyed and brown-haired

Mexicans and Chicanos . . .
   —are happy-go-lucky
   —wear sandals and sombreros
   —play guitars
   —celebrate *piñata* parties as the essence of Mexican culture

Stereotypes commonly accepted by adults and older children

   —are ignorant and lazy
   —have cultures that are inferior to that of Anglos (are "culturally deprived")
   —cannot speak English well (speak with a heavy accent and frequently lapse into Spanish)
   —are present-oriented rather than future-oriented *("Mañana, mañana")*
   —all have large families
   —are all very traditional Catholics
   —are poor
   —have no concept of time, are always late

Mexicans and Chicanos. . .
   —do farm labor or some kind of manual labor
   —are sly (bandito image), try to cheat you

—drink too much
—were born in Mexico
—are migrants

Puerto Ricans. . .
   —are school drop-outs
   —are gang members
   —carry knives and are violent

Blacks (Afro-Americans)

Stereotypes commonly accepted by young children

   —are big and scary
   —have funny, wiry hair
   —fight a lot
   —all look alike

Stereotypes commonly accepted by adults and older children

   —are dishonest and untrustworthy
   —like flashy, loud-colored clothes
   —are not as smart as whites
   —are lazy
   —destroy neighborhoods
   —are all on welfare
   —all drive Cadillacs
   —are overly interested in sex
   —have no sense of family responsibility (men)
   —aren't interested in their children

The racial stereotypes appendix is adapted from Kathleen McGinnis, *Cultural Pluralism in Early Childhood Education* (St. Louis: Parish Board of Education, Lutheran Church, Missouri Synod, 1979), pp. 5–8 (available from the Institute for Peace and Justice, 2913 Locust, St. Louis, MO 63103).

CHAPTER 5

SEX-ROLE STEREOTYPING

We have known Frank for several years. He is the father of several children and works in the construction industry. He was at our home checking on some repair work, and we were talking about our families. We asked how his daughter Linda was doing in college. Linda is an exceptionally good basketball player. She is attending college on a basketball scholarship and plays on the women's varsity team. Frank said she was enjoying both the academic and the athletic parts of college life, "but". . . . And Frank explained the "but." The gym was rarely available for the women's team to practice, the heat was sometimes turned on too low during their games, women's games were scheduled at times that minimized the number of spectators, it was difficult to get uniforms. . . . "It really makes me mad," Frank said.

Even though such blatant examples of biased treatment do not confront us every day, our lives and the lives of our children are very much affected and influenced by attitudes and practices that consign men and women to very specific roles and set up policies and structures to keep them in those roles. In considering sex-role stereotyping, some basic definitions must be laid out. We are using "stereotype" to mean "an untruth or oversimplification about the traits, characteristics, behaviors of an entire group of people."[1] Sex-role stereotyping, then, refers to misconceptions or oversimplifications about traits or behaviors or functions based solely on a person's sex. The stereotypes in our thinking and in our culture are a pernicious legacy to bear, one that does real harm to all of us. It is more than a case of our having attitudes that are based on misconceptions; rather it is a case of those misconceptions being used to keep certain people in subordinate positions.

Our definition of sexism, gleaned from several sources, is "a system of attitudes, actions, and institutional structures that subordinates women on the basis of their sex." Secondarily, sexism also operates in a way that limits, and thereby oppresses, men. But the primary oppression is that which affects women.

The Council on Interracial Books for Children explains this further in their book *Human and Anti-Human Values in Children's Books.* "We see the primary victims of sexism as women because they are subordinated in an institutionalized way, as well as by cultural forces. The sexist oppression of men comes mainly, though not exclusively, from cultural forces. We can therefore define sexism primarily as the systematic oppression and exploitation of human beings on the basis of their belonging to the female sex. Secondarily, we see sexism as the repression of people based on cultural definitions of femininity and masculinity, which prevents both sexes from realizing their full human potential."[2]

Building on those definitions, in dealing with sex-role stereotyping from the perspective of a parent we are trying to achieve three things with our children:

1. We are trying to help them see that their potential need not be limited by their sex in terms of career choices, interests, and, most importantly, the kind of person they are becoming.

2. We are trying to develop in them a critical consciousness of the cultural forces that limit and oppress women and men.

3. We are trying to help them understand what sexism is, how it works in our society, and what can be done to bring about change.

Rationale for a Nonsexist Family Life

The life of Jesus points very clearly to the importance of drawing out the fullest potential in each human being. Jesus treated other people, both men and women, as persons of special potential. He treated women in ways that were different from traditional patterns—Mary and Martha, Mary Magdalene, the woman caught in adultery, the Samaritan woman at the well. Jesus came to fulfill the prophecy of Isaiah—"to loose the fetters of injustice, to untie the knots of the yoke, to let the oppressed go free, and release those who have been crushed" (Isa. 61:1–2). Fighting the oppression of women, lifting the yokes that fall on both men and women because of sexism, was a way of liberating them. And to cooperate with Jesus in that same task today is a way of being part of his liberating mission.

Today, the Roman Catholic church document *Justice in the World* addresses the urgency of fighting sexism when it says, "We also urge that women should have their own share of responsibility and participation in the community life of society and likewise of the Church."[3]

And from the United Church of Christ:

> The issues of family and peace and justice go hand in hand with the concerns of women in church and society. Much of what is happening in the American family and in our society is in response to changing roles of women. Politically, the focusing on family life as an issue is in part a reaction to those changes. The United Church of Christ calls upon the whole church to address the concerns of women and eliminate sexism in church and society. Strong advocacy for the concerns of women and justice, women and the family, and as well, peace and human rights and the elimination of racism and sexism in church and society is backed up by policy of the 1.8 million member denomination.[4]

Specifically then, what can we as parents do to counter sex-role stereotypes and to work against sexism. We are proposing two basic areas to look at:

1. *Ourselves:* our own attitudes, behaviors, and how we relate directly to our children in terms of our sex-role expectations.

2. *The world outside our home:* how we and our children are influenced by forces outside of our home environment and what we can do about that influence.

A Look at Ourselves

All of us grew up in a sexist society, and still live in a world permeated by sexism. There are certainly new levels of consciousness present now; there is "social permission" in many circles to talk about sexism, to complain about it, and sometimes to take action against it. But even with this new level of consciousness, sexism has taken hold of us in so many ways that it is important to take a good look at its manifestations in different parts of our everyday lives.

What we do around the home

The old principle "Actions speak louder than words" has never been more true than in the transmission of values to children. We should make full use of it in everyday situations around the home and their implication with regard to sex-role stereotyping. In two-parent families, or in any family situation in which there is a male role model and a female role model, it is crucial to look at our everyday activities and reflect on how these actions of ours mold our childrens' thinking about what is "appropriate" behavior for men and for women. The following list of questions is drawn in part from Carrie Carmichael's book, *Non-Sexist Childraising.*⁵ Carmichael interviewed a large number of parents who are attempting to raise their children in a liberating, nonsexist way, and her book presents the results of her interviews, along with insights of her own.

WHO DOES WHAT?

Who stays home when the children are sick?
Who calls the sitters?
Who deals with the schools and teachers?
Who shops for the food?
Who prepares the meals?
Who does the dishes?
Who does the cleaning?
Who does the laundry?
Who shops for the children's clothes?
Who soothes and snuggles the children?
Who dresses the children?
Who changes the diapers?
Who gets up in the night for a feeding?

Who takes the children to school?

Who takes the children to the doctor? Dentist?

Who gives out the weekly allowance?

Who disciplines?

Who decides how money's to be spent?

Who earns the money the family uses?

Who makes the decisions about when the children can have the car?

Who makes the decision about what time "to be in from the prom"?

Who coaches the kids' teams?

Who fixes broken toys, bikes, etc.?

Who drives the children to rehearsals, practices, games, etc.?

Who attends games when the children are on the teams?

Who does outdoor activities with the children—sports, sledding, biking, etc.?

Who is the volunteer for school-related activities—scouts, PTA, room parent, etc.?

Who takes care of automobile maintenance?

Who does plumbing repairs, electrical repairs?

Who mends clothes?

Who helps children plan parties or other fun events with friends?

Do our answers to these questions indicate that our home behavior falls into fairly traditional patterns? Do we find we are sharing many tasks? Do we instead find that we are assuming many non-traditional roles? Would we like to change our present mode of operating? The purpose of thinking about these kinds of questions is not to indict all that is traditional; it is only to say that if we want to challenge sex-role stereotyping and sexism itself, we must look at the ways we are accustomed to living and be willing to ask ourselves questions.

When Jim and I (Kathy) answered these questions we discovered that there were many household/child care tasks that we shared, like cleaning, taking the children to the doctor and dentist, driving the children to their activities, soothing and snuggling, disciplining, and others. However, we discovered that many other tasks fell into the traditional molds—Jim does most of the household repair work, auto repair, fixing of the children's bikes; I do the cooking, laundry, mend the clothes, shop for the children's clothes.

A problem we see in our patterns is that the tasks which are nurturing and care-giving (cooking and laundry especially) are also the ones that can be perceived by the children as the "serving roles." They are tasks that fulfill the children's simple everyday needs. So we fear an association, perhaps unstated even in their minds, between women and serving—that it is the job of women to serve others. So we struggle with how to show them on a day-to-day basis that serving need not have a gender attached to it—that the serving roles in the household are to be shared, just as are any other opportunities to nurture and care for each other.

We do not feel that there is a "right way" to divide up household and child-care tasks in the home. Time, skills, levels of enjoyment, are all factors in deciding how each household should run. Another factor is the degree of comfortableness with change that exists in the family. Serveral women who are friends of ours have spoken quite openly about wishing that the division of responsibilities in their homes could be more equitable. They would like not to have the ultimate responsibility for all the running of the house with specific tasks given out to others in the family. They would like that responsibility to be shared. But they feel that their husbands and their families are not at a point where they would be comfortable with any more change. Change is often difficult for all of us, especially when the change is to be in our everyday living patterns, affecting our most unguarded moments, and coming in at times when we are tired and just do not feel like being part of a movement for equality. Sensitivity and a deep level of communication are essential when dealing with issues that touch our deepest emotions, our very sense of who we are. While the same could be said for every topic that we deal with in this book, certainly sex-role stereotyping and sexism demand in the case of a two-parent family that husband and wife be willing to listen to each other. They need to spend the time it takes to work out patterns that are truly freeing *for both* and in which they can support each other.

We will mention later in the chapter some ideas about our own modeling for our children in terms of our interests outside the home. At this point, though, one suggestion for a redirection in home responsibilities comes from a Texas family. Wally and Winnie and their four teenage sons have established "co-responsibility" for household chores. If one son's jeans are not washed, he goes to the person in charge of laundry during that time period, not to Mom who then must track down why the jeans have not been washed. It is a way of getting away from a system where Mom has all the ultimate responsibility.

Language

David and Theresa were sitting at the kitchen table talking about "what they wanted to be when they grew up." David said to Theresa, "Do you want to be a fireman?" Theresa nodded vigorously. At this point I decided to enter the conversation, and said, "Now Theresa couldn't really be a fire*man,* could she? I think we should say fire*fighter.* That's a better word anyway because they do *fight* fires—and both men and women do the work." David looked at me with a sort of bemused puzzlement in his eyes. Then he turned back to Theresa and said, "Theresa, do you want to be a *nurse* when you grow up?"

I suppose the real moral of that story is that parents should know when to stay out of their childrens' conversations, but we felt it was a humorous glimpse at a more serious problem—the inbuilt sexism in language. Terminology that has become almost second nature to many of us needs scrutiny.

First of all, our language is "male-dominated." This means that specifically male terms are used to apply to all people—"man" to mean any person, "mankind" to mean all people, "policeman" to mean any police officer, man or woman. The male pronoun "he," in its indefinite use, is used to mean either a man or a woman.

Some people reply, "What difference does that make? That's nit-picking! Let's talk about real issues."

It is certainly true that sexism and the limiting and slotting of men and women into certain roles is much bigger than a question of which words we use. And yet, our language is a very important part of the bigger picture. The words we use reinforce and daily perpetuate the deeper realities of sexism. By using male terms to mean both men and women we give consent to an exclusion of women, to continuing the idea that men are the ones who really count. We probably are not intending to do this at all, but the effect is the same as if we were!

If we put ourselves in the place of the children, we can see the importance of this more clearly. Young children are simply not equipped to make our adult distinction between "man" the male person and "man" the human person. We had an experience with Tommy when he was eight years old that brought home to us the impact words have on children. The occasion was Martin Luther King's birthday. We were taking about Dr. King with the children and asking them what they had discussed in school about him. Tommy said immediately, "We were talking about how he was working for freedom for all men." Our near automatic response was, "You mean freedom for all men *and women*." "No," Tommy said, "the book said *men,* and it meant *just men*."

We would not try to generalize from that one incident. However, all our experience with young children, along with experiences of primary teachers as reported to us, do force us to the generalization that young children cannot make the distinction between the generic *man* and the use of *man* to mean a male person. Language reflects our thought patterns and behavioral practices and at the same time molds those patterns and practices. If we as parents are concerned about our children's attitudes and behavior, then we need to look at our own language in terms of its effect on those attitudes and behavior. In the case of masculine terminology, we are suggesting that we change our own usage of words—that we find alternatives. The National Council of Teachers of English has published specific guidelines which are helpful as we begin to think about change. These guidelines can be found below as the appendix of this chapter.

Besides these more general guidelines about language, there are also specific areas to be attended to. One is that of colloquialisms and jokes. What do the expressions we use say to children about sex-roles? Do our children hear us telling or laughing at jokes that are demeaning to women—from the "dumb secretary" ones to the "nagging wife" ones to the "mother-in-law" ones? Do we use words like "sweet," "pretty," "lovely," "darling," or "delicate" of our daughters without any counterbalancing references? We realized that we were using words in talking to Theresa that were different from the words we were using in talking to the boys, even as they were babies. We would find ourselves telling Theresa what a pretty little girl she was and telling Tommy and David what big strong boys they were. A simple redirection that we have tried is to go out of our way to praise Theresa for feats of strength and to talk to all three of them about their muscles getting stronger, and so on. Also we have tried to comment on how the boys look—"You're looking especially handsome today," or "You did a good job of combing your hair." Not that we think it is a good idea for any of the children to be overly concerned about appearance; but we feel that the culture will press that concern down more heavily on Theresa than on Tommy and David.

Skills and activities

All children should learn what Dr. Jonas Salk calls "human survival skills"—cooking, laundry, basic housecleaning. We rotate household chores in our home, with the children choosing their assignments. There are no "gender-defined" jobs. Friends of ours with older children have used the same approach in helping them develop a variety of skills. Bob, one father we know, has worked very deliberately with his daughter in auto repair skills, as well as other "fix-it" skills about the house. Both sexes should learn how to pound a nail and use a screwdriver, as well as run a vacuum cleaner and scramble eggs.

Activities that develop children's physical capabilities, like sports and dance, often fall into sex-limited categories. There is still a tendency in many parents to push boys in sports and to direct girls away from sports and toward ballet lessons. Emphatically we say that we see sports as a good activity for boys, and similarly ballet for girls. But we look for the day when children will truly be able to choose according to their own interests, instead of according to what society dictates as appropriate. It is certainly true that girls are much freer to participate in a variety of athletic endeavors than they were in the past, but that freedom is not without its strings and can never be taken for granted, as suggested in the story that opens this chapter. There is much work that needs to be done in the area of athletic opportunities for women, both in terms of attitudinal change and in terms of change in the policies of institutions—the amount of school moneys allotted to women's athletics, for example. Two specific suggestions for parents:

a. Boys and girls should both be encouraged to learn how to throw and catch a ball, climb a rope, swim, and develop all the other basic athletic skills.

b. We can look at our gift-giving practices with respect to our own children. Might we give either a son or a daughter a basketball, a baseball glove, and so on, for a gift? (One year for Mother's Day, Jim presented me with a brand new infielder's glove, because my old one had worn thin from so many years of scooping up grounders.)

A further point should be made about boys and dance: there is nothing incompatible between them. One afternoon Tommy and I were watching a TV interview of the choreographer of the Harlem Ballet Company. As they interviewed him they showed some of the dancers. Tommy's immediate reaction was one of admiration for the strength and agility of the dancers. We talked about how much we would both like to see the company perform. It struck me that Tommy had not as yet been affected by a false labeling of ballet as a "sissy" activity—one boys should not be interested in. There are two resources that bear mentioning here. One is a book for very young children called *Max* by Rachel Isadora, about a young boy who warms up for baseball by being part of a ballet class. The other is a movie we have used with teachers called *Men's Lives* (New Day Films, P.O. Box 315, Franklin Lanes, NJ 07417). This film explores some of the very damaging effects of sex-role stereotyping on young men in our society. It might be available through the public library and would stimulate discussion with older children.

The encouragement of artistic and intellectual pursuits is another area for us as parents to examine carefully. Are we as supportive of our sons as our daughters in developing abilities in painting, drawing, poetry, drama, music, work with a needle, etc.? (A man does not have to be a professional football player like Roosevelt Greer in order to enjoy needlepoint for relaxation.)

On the other hand, are we as encouraging and supportive of our daughters in tough academic fields—science, law, architecture, medicine, economics— as we are of our sons? Do we find ourselves less mindful of explaining to our daughters what makes things go, or how this works when put in combination with that? Do only our sons end up with the chemistry and erector sets? Our son Tommy is very interested in science. One day he came home with some science books from the library. Then as he looked carefully at them, he had his own awareness lesson. He said to us, "Look at this. These books just talk about boys—*Adventures in Chemistry for Boys,* and *Boys' Book of Electrochemistry,*" and he went on to read a few more titles. "That's dumb. Girls can do this, too!" We could not help smiling. It was one of those moments when you think something is taking root!

One problem with a discussion of structured activities, whether it is athletics or music lessons or ballet lessons, is that often these activities have a price tag attached to them which puts them out of many parents' reach. While some interests can be cultivated which are less expensive (children can be encouraged to draw with a crayon and paper), that does not soften the fact that this is another area in which the poor are penalized. Children of the economically poor do not have the same opportunities for growth. As a society we have not committed ourselves to insuring that all children have equal chances to develop their abilities and interests. What that means is that if we are concerned about creating opportunities for our own children to develop free of sex-role stereotyping, we should also push for political and social changes in our communities to ensure that right for all children. So that means we need free or minimal-cost athletic programs, music programs, art lessons, more public parks, and the like, for everybody.

Internal qualities

In addition to skills and interests for our children, a discussion of sex-role stereotyping needs also to address itself to the encouragement of internal qualities. Obviously, the kind of men and women our children become is more important than whether or not they can play the piano or kick a soccer ball. We are referring specifically to qualities that are often sex-classified. Girls are often particularly encouraged to be caring, supportive, nurturing, sensitive people. How? Perhaps through doll play when they are young, through baby-sitting responsibilities as they grow older. Boys are often specially encouraged to be assertive, independent, logical in their thinking, decisive, inventive. How? Perhaps through the kinds of toys they have (from building toys to sports equipment to science sets). Our premise is that these desirable human qualities need to be encouraged in *all* children.

In the development of internal qualities, encouragement does come through toys and activities. However, the most effective encouragement comes through parental modeling. A father who expresses his emotions openly, hugs and kisses his children, listens to his children's feelings, takes care of infant needs, works in the kitchen, is interested in poetry or music or art, says a lot to his children without uttering a word about countering sex-role stereotypes. Similarly, a mother who pursues her own path of intellectual development, expresses her own opinions, does not depend on a man to hammer a nail or pump gas for her, participates in sports according to her own interests, and is supportive of her husband and her children but also asserts her own needs, speaks loudly to her children about breaking down prevalent notions of what men and women are supposed to be.

World Outside the Home

In today's culture dangerous messages are consistently sent to children about what it means to be a man and what it means to be a woman. These messages come in different forms through different aspects of our culture, but we find some basic underlying themes:

To be a woman means to:
   —be a sex object, evaluated by her "measurements"
   —be incapable of tough, analytical thinking
   —be incapable of decisive actions, of being "in charge," of handling emergencies
   —be overly concerned about appearances:
      her own—clothes, hair, makeup . . .
      and of her house—obsession with clean floors, shiny dishes . . . etc.
   —function best in a subordinate supportive role, with a man as the leader
   —have physical strengths that are inferior to a man's
   —be excessively emotional, given to crying, fainting, "falling apart"

To be a man means to:
   —dominate women in general or *a* woman in particular
   —flourish in a highly competitive system: be obsessed with winning, being "on top"

—be judged by the amount of prestige attached to his job or salary

—accumulate material possessions; need to "be seen" with them in tow

—be truly comfortable only when "in control," in a position of authority

—not need or appreciate friendships with other men; be scornful of intimacy in human relationships

—be latently or actually violence-prone, happiest in a violent resolution of a conflict.

Where do these messages come from? How are they supported? What effects do they have on the institutions that shape our lives? How can they be challenged and changed? We will take a brief look at four areas, and attempt to define how sexism comes at us in these areas and what we can do to fight it—in schools, work environments, the media, and books.

Schools

The educational system has an indisputably powerful influence on our children, both on their present behavior and attitudes and in terms of molding them for the future. Schools can participate in sexism in a variety of ways. The participation is not always intentional but the result is the same—the subordination of women and the consequent limiting of development of both men and women. The following questions are adapted from a "checklist on sexism" drafted by the Council on Interracial Books for Children.[6] They are examples of the *kinds* of questions that need to be addressed to schools in mounting a campaign against sexism.

School Board

—Are half the members of the Board female?

—Are fringe benefits such as retirement plans, maternity and/or family leave, insurance benefits, and sabbatical and training opportunities equal for females and males?

Administration

—Are women equally represented and salaried in the administrative positions of both the central administration and the individual schools? (assistant superintendents, principals, assistant principals, department heads, etc.)

Teachers

—Are there as many male teachers as female in the primary and elementary grades?

—Are there as many female teachers as male in the high schools?

—Do teachers avoid imposing such sex-role expectations on children as "Girls love reading and hate math and science," or "Boys shouldn't cry," or that boys can be loud and noisy while girls should learn to control themselves?

Guidance
—Are counselors informed as to the realities of sex discrimination in employment, and do they pass this information on to all students, along with adequate remedies?
—Do counselors encourage and counsel female students to strive for skills and training that will equip them to compete for good paying careers in any field, rather than simply assuming that "most girls get married after high school" and do not join the work force?

Students
—Are females encouraged in math, science, sports, and industrial arts, and males in home economics and commercial classes?
—Are females and males equally encouraged to participate in and equally represented in extra-curricular activities like drama, arts and crafts, musical groups, dance groups, athletics, and student government?

Curriculum
—When ideal instructional materials cannot be found, are teachers trained to detect—and to guide their students to detect—both overt and subtle manifestations of sexism?
—Does a curriculum committee, composed of school professionals, parent representatives (including minority and feminist groups), and student representatives (age permitting), screen all instructional materials before purchase for sexist stereotyping, omissions, and distortions?
—Do materials on classroom walls depict males and females in nontraditional non-stereotyped roles?
—Is a conscious effort made to bring in outside people whose image tends to counteract traditional sex roles—female scientists, engineers, dentists, and plumbers, or male nurses, secretaries, and house-husbands?

Where the answers to these questions is unsatisfactory, parents should press for policy changes. Beyond this, parents can and should increase their own level of awareness about what goes on in the schools through talking with other parents, with teachers, with students themselves, and if possible by actually visiting the school. In trying to work for change in schools we have found that the most effective general strategy is to be willing to help in some of the "nitty-gritty" tasks that fall to parents in all schools. This means bake sales, playground duties, transportation, painting walls, coaching, and so on. School personnel are much more willing to listen to a suggestion or a challenge or a critique from someone who has been attentive to *their* needs.

Ronice Branding, a parent of four children, told us of a particular policy change that she and others were able to effect in their high school. Her daughters were all cheerleaders, and Ronice had some very definite concerns about the harmful effects of any standard cheerleading program—the girls' whole identity being tied to the success of the boys, increasing a sense of dependency, inability, and passivity among the girls. But on top of all this, at this school, any girl who wanted to be a cheerleader had to make a commitment to that activity for the entire school year. Consequently one of Ronice's daughters, who wanted to go out for track, couldn't, without foregoing the opportunity to be a cheerleader during a different part of the school year. That policy was finally changed, as a result of much complaining by students and parents. The policy now allows for a spring squad and a fall squad, giving female students the same seasonal options the male students have. Cheerleading remains, but some flexibility is evolving.

Work environment

Even at an early age children can begin to understand how sexism works in employment. For example, as of June 1978 the average weekly pay for women was $194 a week, for men $339 a week.[7] The pay for minority women is lower than for white women.

Our children have the right to be made aware of these inequalities, this discrimination. Then, as they enter the job market themselves, there is all the more reason for them to have a grasp of what employment realities are. Where sexism is concerned, besides the obvious inequality of pay, there are more subtle pressures on women in the work force—sexual advances, especially from "superiors," not being taken seriously, expectations about appearance (being hired as a "pretty face"), and so on. Young women need to be prepared for this sort of thing, and to feel the support of their family as they attempt to fight it in their own way.

The media

The images of both women and men offered to us by TV are narrow and dangerous, especially for young minds groping to define what it means to be a man or a woman. Answering the following questions for ourselves, and then possibly with our children, could help raise our level of awareness and provide material for discussion with our children.

1. How *many* women have major TV roles? minor roles? Perhaps the family could log its TV watching for a week somewhat as follows:

Name of Show	No. of Male Major Characters	No. of Female Major Characters	No. of Male Minor Characters	No. of Female Minor Characters

2. Treatment of sex and woman's body:
—What percentage of women playing roles on the shows we watch are exceptionally attractive physically? How does this compare to the percentage of men?

—How often are the women characters attired in a sexually provocative way? (e.g., *Charlie's Angels*)

—In how many commercials is a woman's body used as a decoration?

3. What personal qualities reflected through characterizations on TV are shown primarily in one sex? (For example: Leadership: male or female? Compassion: male or female? Clear thinking in emergencies: male or female?)

4. Are women seen primarily as dependent on men, or as capable of directing their own lives?

5. List the occupational roles of men and women as depicted in the shows we see in a week.

6. How often does a man use violence to solve a conflict?

7. Do any of the shows make an attempt to deal with injustice toward women? With changing sex roles?

8. How many times are women made to appear incapable, or intellectually inferior to men?

9. How many times does a man solve a problem for a woman? How many times does a woman solve a problem for a man?

10. How many times are men evaluated according to

—the amount of money they have or flaunt?

—the prestige of their occupation?

—how "tough" they are?

The kinds of stereotypes that are reinforced for adults and for children through TV and other media such as magazines and movies need to be countered. This countering can be done by us as parents in several ways; for instance, by:

1. Helping the children become critical themselves of what they see and read. Using the sexism against itself. Even saying things like "Why do you think they have that woman in that picture?"

2. Talking about the sexism in TV programming.

3. Encouraging the children to read stories and watch TV shows that provide role models opposed to prevalent sex-role stereotypes—for example, the TV special "A Woman Called Moses," the story of Harriet Tubman.

Books

Children's reading material is a powerful messenger about sex roles. We parents do most of the selection of reading material for the very young, and our influence is felt even as the children get older and do more of their own choosing. Here are some practical guidelines for evaluating children's books in terms of sexism.[8]

1. Check the visuals.

a. Are females pictured as often as males?

b. Are females pictured in secondary roles to males—waiting on them, learning from them, being protected by them, following behind? Are there the same number of pictures of males in subordinate roles vis-à-vis women?

    c. Are women pictured in trivial or ridiculous ways?

    d. How many pictures show females in an active role? A passive role?

    e. How many of the visuals show females in a way that emphasizes appearances?

    f. Are men pictured taking care of children? Showing emotion?

2. Check the language.

    a. Is generic male terminology used? (e.g. indefinite "he" for either sex)

    b. In young children's books, are the animals male or female?

    c. Are words used which are demeaning to women? (e.g. "broad," "girls" used of grown women, "nag," "shrew," etc.)

3. Check the lifestyles.

    a. Are women seen in a wide variety of lifestyles, or as confined to certain ones?

    b. Are two-parent families seen as "healthy families" and variations seen as "problems"?

4. Check the heroes.

    a. Are women shown in positions of authority?

    b. Are women shown who have worked and are working for women's rights? (Sojourner Truth, Susan B. Anthony, etc.)

5. Look at the relationships among people.

    a. Do the females function mainly in roles that put them in a position of dependency on males?

    b. Are men and women shown as being mutually supportive of each other?

6. Consider institutional sexism.

    a. Is there any indication in the book of the problems women face in our society?

    b. Is there any indication that solutions to injustice toward women demand more than individual good will—that structures must change?

7. Check the author/editor.

    a. How many of your children's books are written/edited/illustrated by a woman?

    b. Is there an indication in the biographical data that the author has any concerns about sexism or sex-role stereotyping?

Conclusion

Change is not easy. Change undertaken with the support of others becomes more palatable. Change undertaken with understanding and sensitivity can become an enlivening force. We have attempted to spotlight some areas in our life that may need change, from our everyday habits around the house to our selection of books for our children. We want to emphasize the need for patience with ourselves and with others, but also the need for perseverance in our task. The payoff is an important one.

Two very different sources speak eloquently to both the need and the payoff. One is Carrie Carmichael's *Non-Sexist Childraising*. The goal of non-sexist childraising, she states, "is celebrating the myriad differences among girls and boys. It is freeing the child to be whoever or whatever he or she wants to be, not squelching the variations because they do not conform to some arbitrary definition of what a man is, or what a woman is. It is freeing the personalities and helping children to develop the strength to sustain their own differentness in the face of adversity."[9] The other source is a poem in the book *Free to Be You and Me* (a treasury of ideas!) called "The Sun and the Moon":[10]

> The Sun is filled with shining light
> It blazes far and wide
> The Moon reflects the sunlight back
> But has no light inside.
>
> I think I'd rather be the Sun
> That shines so bold and bright
> Than be the Moon, that only glows
> With someone else's light.

APPENDIX ON LANGUAGE GUIDELINES
FOR AVOIDING SEXIST USAGE

1. Alternatives to the generic use of man:

Example

	Alternative
Mankind	Humanity, human beings, people
Man's achievements	Human achievements
The best man for the job	The best person for the job, the best man or woman for the job

2. Alternatives for occupations:

Example	Alternative
Chairman	Coordinator (of a committee or department), moderator (of a meeting), presiding officers, head, chair
Businessman, fireman	Business executive, fire fighter
Mailman	Mail carrier
Steward, stewardess	Flight attendant
Policeman, policewoman	Police officer

3. Alternatives for pronouns:

a. Recast into the plural.

Example	Alternative
Give each student his paper as soon as he is finished.	Give students their papers as soon as they are finished.

b. Reword to eliminate unnecessary gender problems.

Example	Alternative
The average student is worried about his grades.	The average student is worried about grades.

c. Replace the masculine pronoun with "one," or (sparingly) "he or she," as appropriate.

Example	Alternative
If the student was satisfied with his performance on the pre-test, he took the post-test.	A student who was satisfied with her or his performance on the pre-test took the post-test.

From *Guidelines for Nonsexist Use of Language in NCTE Publications* (National Council of Teachers of English, 1111 Kenyon Road, Urbana, IL 61801).

CHAPTER 6

FAMILY INVOLVEMENT IN SOCIAL ACTION

In 1977 a group of concerned Christians, meeting in Detroit, issued a challenge:

> We recommend that all programs dealing with family life, at all levels, in the church, address in a special way the specific education of families in making them aware of the needs of others in their neighborhood, their local communities, or in the world community. These family life efforts will work with other social justice agencies to create environments and develop programs which encourage families to get involved in an action and reflection process in the service of others and the attainment of justice [*The Call to Action,* "Family": II, 1].

Good Friday, 1979, was a special experience for our family in trying to live out this recommendation. At breakfast, we explained to the children why we had decided to withhold a symbolic $12.00 from our federal tax payment—as a protest against increases in military spending and decreases in spending for human needs. The human-need examples we used were simple, ones they were already familiar with and ones we planned to see later in the day.

That afternoon we left work early to spend an hour with the children remembering and responding to the passion of Christ. First, we went to rubble piles next to our office that weeks before had been homes. Then we stopped at the nearby parish school about to close; the children noticed the colorful Easter pictures in the windows and commented on how much the students probably liked their school. What a shame homes are destroyed and schools are closed because tax dollars are going for Trident submarines rather than neighborhood rehabilitation and education was our reply.

The next stop was the children's hospital where David had recently undergone surgery. Each child had decided to bring a book to leave in the playroom. They had talked about how children awaiting surgery often feel afraid and lonely; their books were a response to Christ's suffering in other children. Then, suckers in hand (from David's nurse), we headed off to the post office, where we all signed our tax protest letters and mailed them to the president, the IRS, and our congressional representatives. There we talked about how important it is to try to change the situations that contribute to poverty, as well as to respond to people's immediate needs (though Theresa was more concerned about how to spell her name!).

The last stop on our short journey was the county jail, where a young man we had gotten to know had been awaiting trial for two years. Since the children were tired, we switched plans from individual letters to a group letter to Gerald, which we all signed and delivered to a jail guard. We ended the hour with a prayer for Gerald and his mother—two people experiencing Christ's Passion in their lives.

Rationale for Involving Children in Social Action

As busy people and parents, we would not have time enough both for our children and for some response to Jesus' call to hunger and thirst for justice, if we did not try to combine the two. Some teachers have come to the same conclusion—joining their duty to be with their students with their desire to work for change in their community.

"But why drag younger children along? Aren't you subjecting them to aspects of reality they aren't emotionally or intellectually ready to handle? They'll get enough of evil as they grow up. Aren't you stripping them of the beautiful, the good, and the playful aspects of reality?"

Questions like these are often raised when we speak to parents and educators on "involving children in social action." These questions have challenged us to make sure that we do *not* strip our children of beauty, goodness, and play. But each time we face these questions, we come away more firmly convinced of the value of what we are doing for and with our children.

First, we want (and the world needs) young people, including our elementary school-age children, to be hopeful—and with a hope actually rooted in reality. We want them to know through experience that, difficult as it is, change is possible, and that they can help bring about that change.

But in order to have this realistic hope, this realistic faith, our children must learn how to deal with the actual situations that call for change. Many people are paralyzed by evil. They withdraw into their private worlds because they do not know how to act, what to do. We do not recommend overloading children with social problems. On the contrary, we are trying to help them deal creatively with ones that are all around them. A good dose of this, of course mixed with ample helpings of fun together, nature's wonders, and the beauty of being alive, makes for a fuller young person, not a warped one.

Second, we want our children to experience social action as a regular part of family life, not as something their class does once a year at Christmas or one semester in high school as part of a community-service course. If social action is experienced by children as a "special extra," tacked on if there is time, then it may well remain that way for them as adults. This probably means that it will not be included in their life agenda. But if social action is integrated into the routine of family living, if it is experienced as an integral part of life, then it can be that "constitutive dimension of the preaching of the Gospel" and of Christian living to which the 1971 Synod of Catholic Bishops called us.

There are other reasons for involving children in social action. To build for a moment on Chapter 1 on stewardship, we find that children involved in social action enjoy an experience of a stewardship of their talents and other resources and consequently experience the rewards of giving themselves. One of these rewards is the deep fellowship that comes from working together with others for change. Children's vision of life and of their role in it is broadened.

Finally, the urgency of the world situation demands that the creativity of young people be linked as much as possible to the pressing needs of our communities and world. The world today is more aware of how widespread problems like hunger are. At the same time, we are becoming more aware that these problems need not be, that they are the result of human decisions, that we have the technology to overcome them, and that the institutions of our country and our affluent ways of living are a real part of the problem. Thus, as Westerners living in this reality, we experience an urgency to do what we can to address these institutions and ways of living of ours and to help our children grow to do what they can too. Not to act, and help the children act (or prepare to act later)—is to become part of the problem.

And not to act, as God tells us through the prophets, is not to worship God.

Is not this the sort of fast that pleases me—it is the Lord Yahweh who speaks—to break unjust fetters and undo the thongs of the yoke, to let the oppressed go free, and break every yoke, to share your bread with the hungry, and shelter the homeless poor, to clothe the person you see to be naked and not turn from your own kin? Then will your light shine like the dawn and your wound be quickly healed over. Your integrity will go before you. Cry, and Yahweh will answer; call, and he will say, "I am here." If you do away with the yoke, the clenched fist, the wicked word, if you give your bread to the hungry, and relief to the oppressed, your light will raise in the darkness, and your shadows become like noon. Yahweh will always guide you, giving you relief in desert places. He will give strength to your bones and you shall be like a watered garden, like a spring of water whose waters never run dry [Isa. 58:6-11].

Six Basic Principles

Over the years, as we have involved our children in social action and reflected on this with groups, we have come to some basic principles that underlie our efforts and seem to be especially important in making this endeavor a fruitful one for all of us. While some of the principles overlap, we offer these six separately for your consideration.

Principle No. 1: We regularly invite the children to join us in social action.

We are continually surprised at how much our children (and other children) can understand what we are doing if we take the time to explain it to them. Our Good Friday activities above were a good example. Explaining tax resistance to four-, six-, and eight-year-olds can be a little tricky! But once they were assured that they did not face a jail sentence (Tommy's concern), and once they got clear about whether the president would be arrested for taking $12.00 from our bank account or salaries (David's concern), and once Theresa realized that we would help her sign her name to our letters, they all agreed to sign. Then five people each signing five letters in a crowded post office was time-consuming, but the good feelings we sensed in the children as they pushed the sealed letters through the slot certainly justified our decision to share our action with them and invite them to join us in it.

A good friend of ours related an experience of hers with her nine-year-old son and teenage daughter on the issue of racism. Her Action Against Apathy group had taken on the task of monitoring TV shows and commercials for the frequency of Black characters and for stereotyped images of these Black characters. Instead of doing it alone she invited her children to be part of the activity. Not only was it an enjoyable parent-child experience—an occasion to share information and concerns and life with her children—it was also an opportunity for the children to develop critical thinking skills and a more critical, objective stance vis-à-vis television.

There are a lot of ways in which parents can regularly invite their children to consider social issues. Inviting them to co-sign letters to legislators (as we did), to corporation executives (as we did with a letter to the president of the Nestlé Corporation), or to editors of newspapers—making the letters family letters—is one way.

Some parents occasionally bring their children to social action meetings. Being present in an atmosphere of social action has a way of making children more comfortable with that atmosphere and serves as an implicit invitation to join in the activities. As the children get older, the invitation can be made explicit.

Another suggestion is occasional family discussion of our social concerns. For us, this is generally at mealtimes or at our prayer times. Our discussions concerning two prisoners for whom we have been advocates is leading our children to a whole new awareness and to wanting to help in some way. Those discussions made it easier for us to include the visit to the county jail in our Good Friday activities. We were not sure our children would want to visit a jail, until we asked. But they did. We are also finding our children more responsive as we begin to ask them for their thoughts and feelings (and advice) on what we are doing. Asking other family members for prayers for one's individual social concerns also helps.

We are discovering, though, that this principle of invitation is not as simple as it may seem. Here are four things we and others have learned about this principle.

1. It takes time to explain our doings enough for the children to be able to understand and respond. Our children asked us questions for a full hour when we told them we were going to the jail to put our home up as bond for a prisoner. But it was worth it for many reasons, including their desire to go to the jail with us to do it. Time for hour-long discussions is often a luxury, especially in single-parent situations. How we have come to deal with this is:

—We remind ourselves that this is part of what we committed ourselves to in becoming parents and that it is a very rewarding part of that commitment.

—We emphasize quality over quantity. It is not a matter of how *many* issues we address in a long talk, but how well we care about the one or few that we address.

—We look for discussion opportunities occasionally while riding in the car, waiting in a dentist's office, and so on.

2. The children are free to say no. IF WE SAY "INVITATION," WE HAVE TO MEAN IT. If we coerce them, with threats or rewards, if they feel they will "pay" in some way if they do not want to go—then we have not served their growth (or our social concerns) at all. The more we force them the more they will rebel. The more they join us because they want to, the more internalized their actions become and the more likely they will be agents for social change themselves once they emerge from under our wing.

There are times, however, when parents have expected their children to be part of some social action involvement and have met unanticipated resistance. The recommendation of many friends is to plan the activities for a time that least conflicts with the schedules of family members expected to participate. Principle No. 4, below, bears on these situations, as does the following observation.

3. As far as possible, see that decisions on social action involvement are family decisions. The more the children participate in decisions on the family's social action involvement, the more likely they are to want to participate in the action. This means discussing with them which issues and/or activities to take on. It means involving them in planning and evaluating the activities. It means asking them to identify the roles or functions they are most comfortable with in the activity.

In our family this has evolved into integrating social action into some of our weekly family meetings. At least once a month we add an item to the agenda called "family service." This allows the children to help choose our next activity, rather than its being imposed by us. (We have found it necessary to "structure" into our planning certain aspects of family life we consider essential. Some things do not always happen just by wishing them to, and social action plans will not necessarily come up by themselves just because we consider this sort of planning to be important.)

Now, when we have something we want to do that involves the children in some way, we try to remember to bring it to the family meeting. Our experience as short-term foster parents, as well as the shared experience of other foster parents, has made us careful to ask the children about bringing someone else into our *(and their)* home. If the children feel threatened by the visit in some way, it should be discussed. Perhaps this is not a good time to bring someone else in. Similarly, if some new social action involvement will mean significantly less time to be with the children, then they should be part of that decision. One friend shared with us that her children, now adults, said they had felt she was so busy with her social action work and with caring for other people brought into their home that she did not have time for them. Also, since they had not been part of their parents' decision to live more simply, they had felt they were "kept" poor when they had the money to live differently.

Finally, if you want to be more reflective and systematic about this process as the children get older, Charlie Shedd offers an intriguing tool called "circles of involvement."[1] A group of people each get a sheet of paper with the following design and fill it out according to the accompanying instructions.

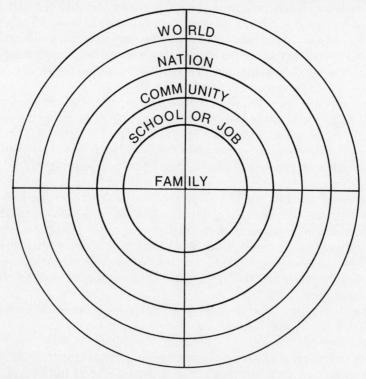

—In the upper right quadrant, write a word or phrase to *describe* your world, nation, community, etc.

—In the lower right quadrant, write a word or phrase to state what you *like best* about your world, nation, etc.

—In the lower left quadrant, write a word or phrase to state *what change* you would like to see in your world, etc.

—In the upper left quadrant, write a word or phrase to state something you *could actually do* to bring about this change.

The completed charts are shared among family members and the search for consensus can begin.

If this tool is appealing and your goal is actually to reach consensus on family social action involvement, we would suggest several refinements. First, do each circle separately, perhaps one circle per family meeting, or one every so many weeks. Then open your general discussion with the circle which generated the most enthusiastic response. Then seek a group desire or action along the lines suggested in the section on family meetings in Chapter 2. A family may decide that with one circle or another no consensus is likely. In that case, the family can encourage those individuals who want to act (alone or together) to carry out their action on their own and report on it to the family afterwards.

4. Involve each parent. The experience of families with older or grown children leads us to recommend that, where there is more than one parent, *both* parents should invite the children to join the social action. If one parent is not involved, the children get different messages. Social action involvement will be perceived as more integral to life, and family life, if it is a shared value and is modeled in some way by each parent. One couple for whom social action was not a shared value suggested that, if at all possible, this difference in values be openly discussed by the family. Sharing with the children their reasons, allowing them to ask questions, and enabling them to see that the non-involved parent nevertheless encourages the involved parent (if this is indeed the case) might reduce the potential for ambivalence and confusion. It might also help the involved parent to feel freer to invite the children to join in the action.

Principle No. 2: Broad exposure to advocates, victims, situations, is crucial.

This is where, especially for younger children, exposure to injustice and the security of goodness and beauty and love need to be found together. But even part of the goodness, beauty, and love to be experienced is in the caring, the struggle, and the humanness of both those who are working for justice and the people who are the victims of the injustice.

For families with children in their teens or twenties, especially if social action has not previously been part of the parents' concern, this exposure is doubly important. In some ways it may be too late for parents to become effective models for their older children; then the parents need to help structure situations in which their children will be touched by others as models, particularly by people close to their own age.

1. Exposing children to advocates for justice is important for at least two reasons. The first is motivation. The witness of people who are giving themselves generously, often at some risk, can help us (young and old) overcome our fears of getting questioned or laughed at or ignored or worse. The witness of people whose motivation is not financial gain offers an important counter-model to the materialism all around us. The witness of people who have translated religious ideals like "peace and justice" into practice shows what a living faith can mean. And the witness of people whose life of service and social change brings them tremendous joy and satisfaction as well as pain and discouragement counters the prevailing myth that only in having is there happiness. Such people demonstrate the truth of God's Word that it is in giving our life away that we find life.

Second, exposing children and adults alike to advocates helps to overcome another obstacle to action—ignorance of what to do and how to do it. The activities of advocates, especially if we have a chance to ask them questions and listen to their stories can give all of us ideas about what we can do. Many of us lack imagination as much as motivation! We need to see a wide range of possibilities when we consider what "action on behalf of justice" can mean for us.

2. Exposure to the victims of injustice has similar benefits, especially in terms of motivation. Statistics about hungry people or the victims of racism often do not touch our hearts and move us to action. However, the experience of a hungry *person* or victim of racism often does. There is an urgency about injustice that we do not generally feel personally unless we encounter its victims.

"It isn't that bad anymore" or "everyone has it rough" are expressions of attitudes that can get in the way. Often it is only contact with a real victim of injustice that can break through these attitudes and mobilize our will and passion as well as our intellect and body.

Further, encountering the victims of injustice, especially in their struggles against that injustice, can break down another counter-productive attitude. Most non-poor and non-victims think of the poor as internally needy and deficient. They are not seen as gifted, as people often quite capable of helping themselves. Experience can dispel this stereotype. It will be pointed out in Principle No. 5 that meeting the victims of injustice in their giftedness can open us to learn from them. And we have much to learn from them, especially about injustice and action for justice.

3. Exposure to a wide variety of situations and places enhances our knowledge and our skills. It opens our eyes, and we begin to see more clearly both the details of specific injustices and the breadth of some of them. It helps us, young and old, to know who and what we are up against. Finally, we learn to be more comfortable in different situations and how to move in these situations. We become more adaptable, less fearful, and thus more effective.

4. Concrete possibilities.

a. Guests in our home. Encouraging advocates or victims, especially if they are friends, to visit, have a meal, stay overnight, and be with our children during some of that time is a natural and therefore important way to expose our children to the realities of injustice and the avenues for combating it. For most people, this means conscious decisions, planning, and a certain amount of unspontaneity at first. The more it happens, however, the more natural it seems to become. A wide variety of opportunities for service is opened up to the children if there is a wide variety of people coming through their home.

b. *Parents themselves.* All the suggestions given in Principle No. 1 offer ways for parents to be advocate-models for their children. This is especially valuable if we as parents convey a "we're in this together" attitude to our children. If we share our doubts or fears, and ask for their advice and prayers, we enable them to identify with us more. Advocates who seem too good, too perfect, do not necessarily inspire confidence in younger people. Maybe that is why God chose parents to be parents. We are all too aware of our shortcomings—so why not acknowledge them to our children?

c. *Reading.* Tommy's fourth-grade teacher has her students reading biographies. In addition to seeking out multicultural heroes as suggested in Chapter 4, we consciously encourage Tommy to read about justice and peace heroes. When we read stories to younger children we can include justice and peace advocates. If we work with older children in a classroom setting, we can encourage projects about these heroes.

d. *TV, movies.* While television generally has a negative impact on children, it offers a couple of positive possibilities in this particular area. Specials and documentaries sometimes detail the lives of victims and advocates. We try to watch some of these with our children, using the commercial breaks, as well as time afterwards, to share thoughts and feelings. Movies, too, can be the occasion of being touched or inspired, as well as times of fun and family togetherness.

e. *Neighborhood.* Street festivals in the inner-city neighborhood where our office is located have provided fun experiences for our children and at the same time have enabled them to encounter victims of injustice working to rebuild their neighborhood and celebrate their community. This contact with our neighborhood and some of its people made our Good Friday visit to the rubble piles of former homes more poignant.

Jail visits, courtroom visits, and visits to the home of our prisoner friend's family have made lasting impressions on our young children and broadened their lives. Serving meals in a Catholic Worker house of hospitality, delivering toys to an inner-city community center, worshipping in an inner-city church on occasion, will allow our children to be touched by reality in a very consciousness-raising way.

f. *Traveling.* Trips offer unique opportunities to experience new situations and encounter new people. Long drives also allow more time for reading and for sharing what is being experienced. Now that our children are reading they are taking over some of the "research" tasks as we travel.

A question from David when he was six showed us the value of what we were doing. Driving through Nebraska up into South Dakota, we noticed a marked deterioration in the quality of the land once we entered the Rose Bud Sioux Reservation. David did too, and asked why. Our explanation of why the worst land would be "reserved" for Native American people made sense to him in a way that it never would have at home.

Principle No. 3: We try to invite the children to actions that are within their capabilities.

We can all benefit from situations that stretch us, challenge our attitudes and concepts and actions. BUT EXPOSING CHILDREN TO SITUATIONS FOR WHICH THEY HAVE NEITHER THE INTELLECTUAL NOR EMOTIONAL CAPACITY MAY DO MORE HARM THAN GOOD. Thus we think it is crucial to seek out those social action possibilities that are best suited for all members of the family. "Best suited" will be defined by a combination of ingredients—how well an action integrates with the interests, skills, knowledge, responsibilities, and time of family members. But no matter what actions we choose, we should take ample time to discuss the issue and action(s) with our children, let them ask questions and give their opinions. As set forth in Principle No. 1, we have to be willing to take this time if the action is to be meaningful to them.

1. Relate actions to home and family living. When our children were pre-schoolers, we centered part of our social action involvement around our home, so that they could share it with us. That was the short-term foster-parent period of our family life. The children came to understand teenagers' need for a home. And the children were an important part of the teenagers' experience as well. All had to make sacrifices and adjust their lives (with an extra person competing for the bathroom, for opportunities to talk at meals, for parents' time and attention). And the children provided a joyful acceptance that teenagers need, as well as an opportunity for the teens to care for them.

In another project, bringing children their own age into the family for a day (giving other parents or resident counselors a much-needed break) offered opportunities for the children to serve by sharing their time and possessions and enjoying other children. Sharing food and toys, sacrificing an occasional treat or event to help another family pay a heating bill—these are precious exercises in understanding people's needs.

2. Build on prior experiences. The selection of our five "stations" in the city in the opening of this chapter was based primarily on what the children had already experienced. The rubble piles and school were on blocks the children had travelled many times. Only two months earlier David had been a patient in the section of the hospital we visited—and happily the same nurse was on duty. Gerald's story and the county jail were not new either. Consequently the children were freer to focus on a new dimension of their old experiences—seeing them in the context of Jesus' Passion and responding to Jesus as he continues to suffer today.

Thus as a general rule we recommend seeking out opportunities for further involvement on issues or with groups with which children have some previous experience. This makes understanding easier and involvement less threatening, and helps assure integration of the experiences into their lives. With teens, if possible, it might be good to consider involvement in issues directly touching teens themselves—military service, inequitable enforcement of the law, drugs, and so on.

Again, the quality of involvement is far more important than the number of issues and actions. It is good for children to learn that victories do not come easily if they come at all, and that it takes time and perseverance to work for change. ("Isn't Gerald out of jail yet?"). Thus, ongoing campaigns like that of the United Farm Workers and the Trident protests and local efforts to work with victims of racism, because of their longer-term character, have balanced some of our one-shot and shorter-term activities.

Moreover, it is interesting and encouraging to see how the children are beginning to explain an issue like the Trident to their friends, now that we have thought of inviting other families to join us. Staying with an issue in the long term can enable children to be resources for other children.

3. Seek out social action opportunities in which children can have a specific role.

Occasionally action campaigns naturally include activities specifically geared to children. Find these if at all possible, or recommend to groups that they include activities that encourage family participation. One year on the feast of the slaughter of the Holy Innocents (December 28), our Clergy and Laity Concerned group (CALC) organized a demonstration at the headquarters of General Dynamics (makers of the Trident submarine) that included children's games, decorating a dead tree with peace cranes, and singing carols, in a festival of life in the shadow of a building where decisions are made about death. Candy canes and gifts of paper cranes for corporate executives added to the holiday flavor and made it an experience the children enjoyed as well as understood.

The children had been encouraged to express that understanding in preparation for the event by making their own signs to carry. This meant an hour with our children before the event. We discussed the meaning of the event, and they formulated and made their signs. Theresa's read: I LIKE SCHOOLS, NOT BOMBS. The presence of other children, especially that of a friend we invited to join us, added to the children's feeling "at home" at the event.

The example of a friend who geared her anti-racist involvement to aspects of the issue her children would understand is instructive. She concentrated on racism in the media and in schools. The media emphasis included the TV monitoring we mentioned in Chapter 4, and this intrigued her son and got him involved. So did the focus on schools. As the issue became a topic of informal conversation at home the children's interest increased. Eventually this enabled the children (one in elementary school and one in secondary) to bring home their observations of racism at their schools. Later it led to overt action by the children themselves, with parental support.

By way of contrast, another friend shared with us how her own extensive social action involvement was never planned with her children in mind and was beyond their capabilities. She concludes that this is the reason her children never participated at the time and have never exhibited any real concern for social action later as adults and parents themselves.

4. Recognize and respect children's limits. Our Good Friday outing was limited to five "stations," and we cut the last one short. We have recommended above taking seriously any reservations the children might have about bringing a new person into the home and making social action decisions and planning a family matter. We do not want the children resenting social action. We feel it is important not to push them beyond their limits.

Our experience has confirmed us in our caution. In the summer of 1977 we were teaching in Seattle and had decided to celebrate the Fourth of July by joining the Pacific Life Communities in a protest at the future base of the Trident submarine. A ferry ride and long drive meant leaving before dawn. By 10 A.M. the children were tired, but we had only begun preparations for the action. It was clear that we would never last until 3 P.M. except by coercion. Once we realized how irritated we were becoming with the children, we caucused and created an alternative plan: Tommy, with assistance from the rest of us, would make a big poster which we would take back and display in the dormitory at Seattle University as our family statement on "LIFE WITHOUT TRIDENT." Then it was off to a nearby beach for the rest of the day. As adults wanting to share in the fellowship and inspiration of the full day, we were disappointed. But as parents interested in the long-term effects on our children and committed to genuine family action, we felt we were making a good family decision.

Principle No. 4: We try to integrate fun whenever possible.

Parents want their children freely to choose their own values and way of life. If we are offering an alternative way of living to our children, they should see it as attractive—difficult, perhaps, but full of meaning and joy. Working for justice and peace need not and ought not always be a solemn, painful struggle. In the Good Friday episode, Tommy made an interesting comment as we were walking into the hospital ("station" #3). "Why does all this have to be so bad?" he asked, implying that we had loaded him with problems in the first twenty minutes. Luckily the nurse provided suckers and balanced the experience for him.

There are many ways we can build enjoyment into social action involvement. Among them:

1. Combine action with a fun event, as in the Bangor/Seattle beach trip above. Family celebrations of days like Martin Luther King's birthday can combine some social action with traditionally fun elements like a birthday cake (and perhaps a filmstrip for children on Dr. King or Rosa Parks). Taking another child into the home for a day might help constitute a fun activity. Or at Christmas time this might mean a drive into the country to chop down a Christmas tree together.

2. *Join with others, especially other families.* Community is fun. Doing your social action with others, like inviting other families to cook a meal at a Catholic Worker or other house of hospitality, makes social action more attractive. The support and challenge of a community is absolutely essential for nurturing one's commitment to justice and peace and is one of the biggest joys of this way of life. As Jesus promised: "There is no one who has left house, brothers, sisters, father, children or land for my sake and for the sake of the gospel who will not be repaid a hundred times over, houses, brothers, sisters, mothers, children, and land—not without persecution—now in this present time . . ." (Mark 10:28–30).

3. *Put consciousness-raising into an enjoyable context.* Meals with advocates, celebrations of birthdays or feasts of people like Dr. King, Saint Francis, or Gandhi, movies with a message, and street festivals in inner-city neighborhoods, have already been mentioned. A Holly Near concert is a powerful experience for older children. Her tapes and records, and those of others like Pete Seeger and Buffy Saint-Marie, are instructive as well as entertaining.

4. *Involve the children in doing and making.* Creatively expressing their values on placards of their own making is one way. Helping prepare a meal for the Catholic Worker house, baking bread to take to a shut-in, and even as simple an activity as operating the filmstrip projector at a social justice educational event, can all make the children feel more useful and the experience more enjoyable.

Several families in a local United Church of Christ congregation spent three Saturdays last Lent involving themselves in just such "doings." From 10 A.M. to 3 P.M. they baked bread (fifty-five loaves at a time); the proceeds from selling the bread sent three goats to the Philippines via the Heifer Project. During lunch the group did sections of the *Those Who Hunger* program (see Resources), which carried over into the discussions around the oven. The key for many of the participants, especially the ten- and eleven-year-olds, was the physical activity—baking the bread![2]

Principle No. 5. Social action involvement means "doing with" rather than "doing for."

Doing justice means respecting and promoting the dignity of others. This in turn means working with people in such a way that their own value or giftedness is recognized, affirmed, and called forth. "Helping" others needs to be seen more as "doing with" others than "doing for" them. Service is like gardening.

> And we are gardeners for these flowering hopes; for to garden is not to give life but to tend life—to empower to leaf and flower the sacred seed in each.[3]

Helping someone, then, should as much as possible mean working to enable that person to develop and contribute his or her own unique gifts to the human family, the Body of Christ.

There are many ways to build more mutuality or reciprocity into our social action involvement. But especially, we should:

1. *Allow ourselves and our children to be resourced by "needy" people.* The poor are more than their poverty. The disabled are more than their disability. The elderly are more than their weakening bodies.

The elderly members of one's own family—the grandparents, for instance —provide an excellent opportunity for children to "garden." That is, children can ask questions, listen to grandparents' stories and insights, learn skills from them, and work with them (picking and canning fruit, repairing, reading, sewing, carpentry, gardening). And they can receive as well as give attention and companionship. As parents, we do both our children and our own parents a real "service" by fostering a reciprocal relationship between them.

Preparing, serving, and eating a meal with the guests at a Catholic Worker house offers another, though more difficult, opportunity for children and adults to relate with, and often to learn from, people whom society considers outcasts. Worshipping in an economically poor church on occasion allows us to be resourced by the faith of the congregation. A family doing this could hope to get to know at least one family from that congregation and set up a reciprocal relationship whereby both families could learn from and contribute to each other. The suggestions in Chapter 4 on seeking the services of minority professionals is yet another way to break down the stereotypes most white people have about people of color being "needy."

2. *Set up exchanges whenever possible.* Some of the most popular hunger actions—like Thanksgiving and Christmas food baskets and food collections for food distribution centers—are difficult to make mutual, since they are generally "one-shot" efforts. But if a relationship can be established with a single family, as suggested above, genuine exchange is easier to effect.

Families can pair with a family overseas too, through the mission agencies of our churches. An exchange of letters and pictures can provide real moral support for both families' efforts to work for justice. The global, as well as the local, consciousness of our children needs to be nurtured.

Family members, individually or as a group, can correspond with a prisoner and be touched by, as well as touch, that person's life. This had been so eye-opening and heart-stretching for us as adults the past four years that we decided recently to invite our children to join us. We chose Valentine's Day as our launch date because concern for prisoners is the origin of that celebration. The Sunday before February 14, while the children were making valentines for their grandparents, we told them of the tradition that on the eve of his execution in the year 270 the original Valentine wrote a note to his jailer's daughter thanking her for her friendship during his imprisonment—and signed it "Your Valentine."[4] We also told them about Standing Deer, our friend in prison, and they decided to make him a special valentine using their school pictures.

Standing Deer's response touched us even more than our children had apparently touched him.

> Tell the kids I loved their Valentine's card with their pictures and I have it on my picture board on my wall. You needn't tell them it made me weep because big strong convicts don't do those things, but I did. I was so emotionally moved by the beauty of you all. If your God produces folks like you and your family, He and Tunkashila Wakan Tanka are without doubt one and the same, and Chief Seattle was right.

As a resource for finding names of prisoners who want outside correspondence, the *Alternative Celebrations Catalog* recommends writing Prison Pen Pals, Box 1217, Cincinnati, OH 45202.

Some parishes have begun to pair up and organize suburban/inner-city exchanges. Instead of the non-poor always being the giver, the tutor, the coach, whatever, an exchange of dramatic or musical performances or of family education programs between inner-city and suburban church groups is arranged. Others have developed a community vegetable garden. There is nothing like working with your hands side-by-side with people to break down barriers of inequality. Church land and vacant lots can make excellent community gardens. On a smaller scale, two families, one from each of these paired churches, can plant a common vegetable garden.

3. Promote self-help efforts. Relating with the economically poor and other victims precisely in their creativity, in their efforts to organize and support themselves, can be a powerful lesson for us, while promoting the victims' dignity as well. For instance, we might encourage our children to buy the handicrafts of the economically poor. (And we might do the same ourselves.) The *Alternative Celebrations Catalog* (see Resources) contains excellent lists of self-help centers and other sources for these products. Churches often have Christmas bazaars where elderly members display and sell their foods and handicrafts.

Or we might offer our resources as a family to a neighborhood organization or church where we know the people themselves are working to improve their community. The more we get into the habit of saying: "Here we are, with the following skills, contacts, and time. Can you use these resources? If so, how?"—the more genuinely helpful we will be.

Principle No. 6. Social action involves the works of justice as well as the works of mercy.

Social action means more than caring for victims. It also means working with victims and others to change the political, economic, and cultural situations and institutions that victimize them. As Isaiah put it, the kingdom means breaking unjust fetters and undoing the thongs of the yoke.

As someone else put it more recently, if we want to love our neighbor effectively we need "two feet" to walk the path of service. One foot represents the works of mercy (direct service) and the other the works of justice (social change). As presented in our Lenten hunger program—*Those Who Hunger*—the feet look like this:[5]

THE TWO FEET OF CHRISTIAN SERVICE

For most of us, social action has probably meant simply the works of mercy. Only recently have the works of justice been emphasized. Consequently most of us have little experience with changing institutions and policies. And so in our own family we consciously look for opportunities to integrate the works of justice with the works of mercy. In our Good Friday example, the tax resistance was an attempt to influence a change in federal budget priorities. The discussions at the rubble piles and school included consideration of existing federal priorities as an institutional contributor to poverty.

One way to integrate these two aspects of service is to raise questions with the children about *why* the people we help are hungry or cannot pay their enormous winter heating bills. The discussion might extend to some of what needs to be done to change the *situation,* and how we ourselves could help address the guilty causes or structures. Recall David's question about the quality of reservation land as we entered the South Dakota reservation; it provoked a rich discussion. Similarly, the drive home from any "mercy" activity might be a good time for a "justice" discussion.

Fund raising appeals present another opportunity to discuss and implement the importance of both the works of mercy and the works of justice. Jacqueline Haessly suggests involving the whole family in determining the criteria for whom to support and how much to give (a combination of mercy and justice is best).[6] The more concrete such discussions can be made, the better. For instance, we were fortunate to have in our home the Chilean wall-hanging mentioned in Chapter 3. We used it as a way of explaining the appeal we received to help a Chilean day-care center serving the wives and children of some of Chile's political prisoners. Our children were much more interested and responsive to this concrete approach.

A number of works of justice have already been mentioned. Chapter 1 on stewardship identified ways of resisting, and working to change, some of the structures of materialism in our society. Chapter 4 presented various possibilities for challenging institutional racism. The General Dynamics examples in the present chapter suggest ways of resisting militarism. Inviting the children to co-sign our letters to legislators and corporate executives (or send their own letters) is still another way.

1. Economic action possibilities are numerous. Grocery shopping presents several possibilities. Children can learn important lessons about the responsibility and power of consumers if we take the time to explain about a boycott of Nestlé products or non-union lettuce, for example. Such a discussion could lead older children to think beyond their own food pantry to their school cafeteria or candy machine, and how they might extend a boycott to their school or club. If this kind of awareness were more widespread we might not have had the situation in our neighborhood where a YMCA Indian Guide group was selling Nestlé candy bars to raise money for hungry children in the Third World!

Similarly, trips with the children to a farmers market or to local farms to get fruits, vegetables, and eggs, are an ideal time to talk about how we can empower small farmers in the face of the growing giant "agribusiness" corporations—by buying directly from the small farmers.

Older children have gone to bakeries in some cities to inquire about what was done with left-over goods at the end of a day. In some cases children have distributed, with the help of a person working directly with the hungry, bakery goods that were previously thrown away.

2. Likewise, there are many opportunities for political action. First, there are the consciousness-raising experiences in which children over eight or nine years of age could be included—city council meetings, Public Service Commission hearings on utility rate increases, a visit to the State Capitol for a legislative debate on an issue like welfare rights or the ERA. Family letters to legislators and newspaper editors have already been suggested.

One group of ten- and eleven-year-olds, with help from their teacher and some parents, organized a table outside church one Sunday morning to collect signatures on a petition to include the repeal of Missouri's sales tax on food and medicine on the 1976 ballot. Their class had been discussing the needs of the elderly and some of the *structures* contributing to the poverty of many elderly people. When they realized that this sales tax fell heaviest on those with fixed incomes and with the greatest need for medicine, they decided to extend their Lenten service work beyond doing chores for the elderly in their town, beyond the works of mercy. After the Sunday masses, they invited the adults over to the booth to sign the petitions, while their own parents, as registered voters, served as witnesses to the signatures. And so they walked the path of service with both feet—mercy, yes, but justice too.

Family political action was encouraged in our own parish as a result of a parish Lenten program on hunger. Every couple of months some piece of anti-hunger legislation was brought to the attention of the parish. Bulletin inserts, lengthier written descriptions waiting in the vestibule, and a couple of parishioners at coffee and donuts to provide more information were the steps we used in encouraging parishoners to write their letters to legislators and bring them to church the next Sunday. A letter was sent to all parishioners explaining the activity and providing guidelines on how to write an effective political letter. An empty basket into which the letters were to be placed was the symbolic reminder of our need to do the works of justice, just as the empty grocery bags in church were the reminder to bring canned goods to help directly feed the hungry. Knowing that other parishioners were involved was an incentive to many people to write and bring their letters. It was also an incentive to us to involve our children.

Three Prerequisites for Involving Children in Social Action

The point of this chapter is not just to suggest a variety of ways of involving children in social action. Our goal is not just to multiply the number of children doing social action or the number of actions they are doing. There are certain basic concerns that parents ought to consider in promoting the *quality* of their children's involvement. Here are three prerequisites which we have learned by experience are crucial.

1. Promoting our children's self-esteem and self-confidence

People will not reach out to others or take risks unless they feel good about themselves, confident of their worth and abilities, and supported. This is as true of adults as it is of children. The affirmative environment stressed in Chapter 2 bears fruit here. The more we help our children recognize and develop their skills, help provide experiences and an environment where children find success and enjoyment, and help them learn to discipline themselves and concentrate on their tasks, the more likely they are to pursue a life of service, "walking on both feet."

Especially instructive in this regard is the educational model developed by Mahatma Gandhi for India and still found in "Gandhian schools" in India today. Included in the curriculum is a half-hour public presentation every day for every age level. In this way, at least five times a year each child makes some public presentation at the daily assembly. Gandhi wanted to educate a nation of people able to stand up for what they believed, to stand up in public and not be embarrassed and speechless, to overcome the fears that keep people from acting courageously. We can imitate the spirit of this in many ways. Encouraging our children to act publicly—like reading during worship services, availing themselves of dramatic and musical opportunities, writing a letter to an editor, standing at a public vigil, wearing a button on their shirt or coat—helps them develop confidence in themselves.

2. Relating to our children's needs and interests

Whatever impressions this chapter might have given about the amount of social action we engage in with our children, this is not the only thing, or even the primary thing, we do with them. Most of our time together is simply focused on their needs and interests. We have already reported the warnings of an activist parent whose children felt their parents were too busy to care about them. The more willing we are to go to our children's school plays and soccer games, the more willing we have found them to go with us to the Catholic Worker and General Dynamics.

Being present to our children's concerns means being mentally, as well as physically, free to focus fully on them. This has required us to say no to a number of important projects and efforts. On the other hand, like other families, we are finding that the more our social action involvement is based on the principles discussed in this chapter—especially Principle No. 3 on finding social actions within children's capabilities and Principle No. 4 on making them fun—the more our social action is becoming a genuine need and interest of our children. Generally such involvement provides a big dose of togetherness, creativity, and excitement.

3. Helping our children develop as caring persons

In one sense, it does not matter if our children know about Trident submarines or hungry people in India. More basic than exposing children to *specific* social problems are our efforts to help them develop as caring persons. The more they care, the more they are likely to respond with a growing awareness of social problems and people who are hurting. This is the education of the heart that Gandhian schools stress. There are many possibilities for action here. To mention a few:

Gandhian schools have no cooks or janitors or gardeners. Students raise their own vegetables, prepare their own meals, and clean their own classrooms and dormitories. These are lessons in caring—caring for the earth, for the precious resource of food, for common property. Students learn experientially that we are all called to serve, and not to be served.

Pets are a way for children to learn what is involved in daily, long-term caring. Jobs are another help. One parent has reflected with us on how much her teenagers have learned through work, especially when they were asked to pitch in and work extra to get an urgent task done. Involving the children in family financial decisions, as suggested in Chapter 1, can also promote this development of the heart. And especially, the times when we remember to open our own hearts with our children—sharing our joys and pains in working for change, in being with others, in caring for our children and each other—these times can touch their hearts with deep and lasting good.

Finally, and probably most effectively, extended-family situations afford children regular opportunity to grow into caring persons. "Extended-family" includes of course the grandparents and others who are interacting regularly with the children, whether they live in the same home or not; but "extended family" also means the "strangers" to whom the family opens its home when they need acceptance and love as well as a place to sleep and eat. And finally, the "extended family" can also be a wider community: several families and perhaps some single people sharing their lives more and more with one another. This can nurture caring in young people tremendously. Elise Boulding, a mother-activist-scholar who has lived this more deeply than most of us ever will, strongly recommends such extended family situations:

> For the family to fulfill all its potentialities for nurturing open, loving persons free to carry out radically new missions in an aching society, some equivalent of this extended family is necessary. No family can do this alone.[7]

It is such family/community situations that give many of us hope as we reflect on the kind of life and world to which we are introducing our children. Cathy Stentzel, a member of such a community, put it beautifully in "An Open Letter to My Children" (ages ten and seven), in *Sojourners:*

Sometimes I worry about you; I worry that by bringing you to demonstrations, expecting you to march and sing, or to be silent holding a candle, I am thrusting you into a truth, an anxiety, that you are not old enough to bear. At those times I pray that you are being prepared to understand and be strong—that our life together in the community will make a difference in your lives.[8]

Conclusion

But six principles and three prerequisites are not enough to change the world, or even change our children or ourselves. When it comes to social action, many of us feel as if we were the children. Sometimes we do not know what to do. More often we know what to do but are afraid to act. We look for others to help us understand more accurately what needs to be done. We look for others to help us act more courageously.

But we also need to stop and listen to what our God told Jeremiah when he protested that, as a teenager, he was only a child and was not ready for a prophet's responsibilities. God simply reminded him that it was God who called him and who would walk with him. And that was enough for him. It should be enough for us too. For it is to us, too, that God has spoken:

"Before I formed you in the womb I knew you; before you came to birth I consecrated you; I have appointed you as a prophet to the nations." I said, "Ah, Lord Yahweh; look, I do not know how to speak: I am a child!" But Yahweh replied, "Do not say, 'I am a child.' Go now to those to whom I send you and say whatever I command you. Do not be afraid of them, for I am with you to protect you—it is Yahweh who speaks!" Then Yahweh put out his hand and touched my mouth and said to me: "There! I am putting my words into your mouth. . . ."

"So now brace yourself for action. Stand up and tell them all I command you. Do not be dismayed at their presence, or in their presence I will make you dismayed. I, for my part, today will make you into a fortified city, a pillar of iron, and a wall of bronze to confront all this land: the kings of Judah, its princes, its priests and the country people. They will fight against you but shall not overcome you, for I am with you to deliver you—it is Yahweh who speaks" [Jer. 1:4–9, 17–19].

CHAPTER 7

PRAYER AND PARENTING FOR PEACE AND JUSTICE

It was our turn to host the home liturgy. Since it was the first week of November, we chose a theme which might have been titled "All Saints—Becoming Saints through Service." We had called the other three families and asked them to prepare their children to tell the stories of their own saints, or persons for whom they were named, during Mass. We had also invited a friend from the Catholic Worker house to tell us about her work and how we might help.

At dinner the night before, we talked with our children about their patrons. With Mother Teresa about to receive the Nobel Peace Prize, everyone was interested in Theresa's great namesake in India. David, too, had an interesting story to tell: he was named for David Darst, a relative and early Vietnam-war draft resister, one of the Catonsville Nine.

Tommy, however, was more of a challenge. He informed us right away that he did not want to tell the story of "that one Thomas—he was the only one, after Jesus rose from the dead, who didn't come to the meeting!" (Missing meetings, apparently, is seen as a grave matter in our family!) So we told him about Thomas More. We could tell we had hit on the right Thomas—at least as far as curiosity was concerned. While David was preoccupied with what they did with Thomas More's head, Tommy focused on why he lost his head. The recorded reasons did not seem sufficient justification for sacrificing one's head; Tommy was clearly in less than total admiration of Thomas More's practical judgment.

The next evening at Mass, Tommy was the last of the children to tell their stories. After faithfully recalling the highlights of Thomas More's life and death, he concluded, "But I wouldn't have done it!" Then there was a lovely irony. At that point in the Mass we put on a record and listened meditatively (through the laughter) to the Saint Louis Jesuits singing "Be Not Afraid."

Rationale for Integrating Prayer and Social Action

As the story indicates, we are clearly at the point of planting seeds. Leafing and flowering may be years away. Religious development is slow. We realize that we are ourselves only beginners in integrating prayer into our lives. And

112

not many of those we interviewed for this book had really very much to say about this aspect of parenting for peace and justice.

Thus, while we feel more and more strongly as time goes by about the need to integrate prayer into our family life and social action involvements, we must confess to a thinner experiential base for what we write here than for our preceding chapters. Nevertheless we hope the fruits of our reflection may help spark other reflection and some practical applications for other families.

Basically, we see four reasons for combining prayer with family social action.

1. We need to experience social action as part of the very substance of our faith.

The divorce of spirituality from social action, or of faith from good works, has in the recent past produced both some burned-out activists and some navel-gazing contemplatives. We want our children to experience the unity of the two aspects of the Christian life. We want prayer to be experienced as a part of social action. We want our social action involvement always to be seen in relation to our faith. The more we—children and adults—experience social action as a call from Jesus, and as our response to God's great love for us, the more likely we are to persevere in it.

Prayer, especially silent prayer, allows us to feel the presence of Jesus, to know that we are loved and graced. And the more we sense Jesus' love and gifts, the more we realize that he is sending us forth to share that love and those gifts. This kind of silent openness to Jesus, especially when coupled with group/family reflection, can help all of us discover God's ways in our lives—what Jesus wants of us.

2. We need to know that Jesus walks with us.

The prophet's life, a life of working for justice and peace, is difficult and sometimes risky. Isaiah was afraid. So was Jeremiah, and he asked Yahweh to wait a few more years before drafting him. Gandhi was afraid, especially in his youth. What enabled these prophets to overcome their fears can enable us to take the next step in acting on behalf of justice: "Yahweh will always guide you, giving you relief in desert places" (Isa. 58:11). "Do not be afraid, for I am with you to protect you—it is Yahweh who speaks" (Jer. 1:8). "And know that I am with you always; yes, even to the end of time" (Matt. 28:20). Their faith that God walked with them gave the prophets tremendous courage.

Meditating on the death and resurrection of Jesus (and presenting this in ways our children can begin to understand) helps us discover the appropriateness of our own struggle for justice. The failures we experience—those little "deaths"—and the joy, love, and hope we experience in our struggle for justice—those little "resurrections"—are our way of following Jesus on his way to Jerusalem, to the cross, and to the resurrection. And there are times when all we can do is, like Mary, stand beneath the cross and pray. We want our children to learn this truth with us.

3. Prayer unites us with the whole Body of Christ.

The social actions we do should flow more and more out of an inner bond or oneness with others. These others are Jesus and his whole Body, the human family. This oneness expresses itself in external action—the works of justice and the works of mercy; but it is built in part by prayer, and especially by the Eucharist. The more we pray with and for the members of the Body of Christ, the more this interior oneness is realized. Without this bond, risky action will not last long. "Why bother? Who needs all that hassle, anyway? It's not worth it!" And it's not, either—unless there is this growing unity and love. Thus, we want as a family to begin to experience the unity with the Body of Christ through prayer.

4. Prayer deepens family unity.

We were brought up on the principle that "the family that prays together stays together." This took forms we complained about as teenagers, but some of it stuck with us. Now we are coming back to it as parents. We are beginning to discover the wisdom there is in the advice of people like Elise Boulding, who have learned from experience that a family's willingness to work together—from consensus decision-making through social action involvement—is nurtured in a special way by family prayer or worship.[1]

Five Aspects of Integrating Prayer and Social Action

1. Helping children develop a personal relationship with Jesus

A personal relationship with Jesus is a good in itself, and fostering it in our children is one of the most important aspects of our vocation simply as parents. But it is also part of the foundation of parenting for peace and justice. Courage is one reason for this, as we have explained. A second reason has also been stated: we want our children to experience the call to justice and peace as a call from Jesus. Thus, in order to prepare them to be receptive to this call, we want them to know Jesus personally, know him as their friend and Lord.

In reflecting on how to promote this personal relationship with Jesus, we are in deep, grace-filled, water. We do not presume to know how the grace of God works, through us, through others, through the Spirit's promptings in our children's hearts. Nevertheless, there are some ideas that make sense to us, that our limited experience leads us to suggest as possibilities for others.

Modeling is probably more essential here than anywhere else. Without the witness and sharing of our own personal relationship with Jesus, anything we might say on the subject would be meaningless. This sharing can take place in a variety of ways and settings. The spontaneity of family prayer at meals, at the crib at Christmas time, in front of a warm fire, is especially rich for children's understanding, when we address Jesus directly as friend and Lord. Calling on Jesus aloud—for help at the beginning of some endeavor, or thanking him afterwards—witnesses to this personal relationship. In our family, bedtime prayer with each child individually is the most comfortable setting for this intimate conversation with Jesus.

Inviting the children to pray to Jesus when they need help has always seemed to us a natural way to promote their personal relationship with him. However, there have been times when we wondered if we were getting the real point across! Tommy in kindergarten had an eye operation and had to wear a patch three days a week. He really tried hard, but one morning it just seemed too much for him. Consolingly we talked about asking Jesus for special help that day, and in the evening we asked how it had gone with his prayer. Instead of referring to Jesus and the eye patch, Tommy related how he and a friend were "fooling around in gym class so Mr. Stricker made us run laps." Then in the same breath and with real feeling, he said he had prayed to Jesus to drop a bucket of water on Mr. Stricker's head! So much for our profound thoughts on prayer. So much for the preoccupation with the eye patch, too, though, and we chose to interpret this episode as a step forward in Tommy's religious development. God's ways are not our ways.

Another helpful exercise has been reading the Arch Book (Concordia) New Testament stories with each child. We began this weekly practice once Tommy turned three or four and could finally sit still for ten to fifteen minutes. (This is a monumental feat for our three scramblers.) We refer to the books as "Jesus books," and occasionally we would pray together after reading a story. As Tommy learned to read, he was quite happy to read "Jesus books" with us, alternating pages. Now David is beginning to do the same.

Sunday Mass offers still another opportunity. While this has been one of our most trying situations, the grace of perseverance (and flexibility) has also been given to us on many an occasion. Whispered commentaries by Mom and Dad have become standard practice. At the Offertory we talk with the children about one gift—one thing we will do that day or week—that each of us can give to Jesus to give to God. At Communion time, we usually share a short reflection on receiving Jesus and praying to him within us right afterwards. The effectiveness of our conversation cannot be measured or proved, but we believe that it is all part of allowing Jesus to become a friend and member of our family.

As the children get older, we are finding how important peer influence is. The more a child experiences prayer and "Jesus talk" with other families, and especially with other youth, the more normal it will be seen. For us the monthly home Mass with three other families has been very helpful. So too have been those special few Sundays when we have gone camping with friends. Praying and singing together—on a beach, at a lake, or in the woods—has touched our children, we believe, in a special way.

Environment makes a difference at home too. Is there a "space" for prayer? That is, does the schedule allow some unhurried moments, or is everyone just too busy? Also, is there a place that inspires reflection and prayer? A friend (Elise Boulding) challenges the hectic pace we often allow ourselves to get caught in:

> The anchoring in the divine milieu that can take place in family settings depends on being able to conceive the home as a temple for listening, a place for individual solitude and group quiet. Since solitude and quiet are in general the last thing we look for at home, creative imagination has to be brought into play here. Designated quiet corners in the home, even when there is not enough space for a separate listening room; listening together in silence before meals, by candlelight for a few minutes before bedtime, creates a kind of openness and attunement that is strangely akin to play, and yet delicately centered in a way that play is not. The openness is both horizontal and vertical—to God and to others. The family that sets a high value on "listening silence" helps put its members in touch with the inward teacher and nurturer of that spirit that takes away the occasion of war.[1]

2. A sense of wonder in children: the inner core of stewardship

To expand on the citation just above, we are discovering the place of wonder and reverence in parenting for peace and justice. Wonder and reverence for the earth leads quickly to wonder and reverence for its Creator. It also leads to deeper respect and reverence for people. As Chief Luther Standing Bear put it negatively a century ago: "Lack of respect for growing, living things soon leads to lack of respect for humans as well." The positive statement of this truth is beautifully expressed in the following excerpt from a family religious education program:

> The early years of children are those in which their power and sense of wonder is one of the tools available to parents for directing the religious growth of their children. Children's sense of wonder is nurtured through discovery, sharing, delight, reverence, silence and surprise, which are all a part of each child's daily experiences. . . .
>
> By encouraging children's growth in wonder and reverence, parents are preparing them to become concerned about the world for which they will some day share responsibility. This vision of life will enable children to become loving, responsible, sensitive persons, mature Christians, who believe in the goodness of God and of others.[2]

As this statement implies, the seed of children's sense of responsibility and stewardship for the world is planted and watered when we nurture wonder and reverence in them. Present, silent, prayerful before the beauty of creation, we all grow in awareness that it is gift, a gift from God who loves us personally and intensely, and who calls us to care for and share this gift. The more we experience life as gift and all that we are and have as gift, the more likely we are to share our talents and possessions.

Present, silent, prayerful before the beauty of creation, we all grow in awareness that we are all one, that all is connected. Returning to Chief Seattle (Chapter 1): "This we know. All things are connected, like the blood which unites one family. All things are connected. Whatever befalls the earth befalls the children of the earth."[3]

Present, silent, prayerful before the beauty of creation, we all grow in our awareness that we are one with future generations, that we have a responsibility to care for the earth and use its resources in such a way that future generations can enjoy them too.

This is the heart of stewardship and solidarity. This is the "environmental ethic" as seen from the inside. Pope Paul VI put it poetically in his Encyclical *On the Development of Peoples:*

> Civilizations are born, develop and die. But humanity is advancing along the path of history like the waves of a rising tide encroaching gradually on the shore. We have inherited from past generations, and we have benefited from the work of our contemporaries; for this reason we have obligations toward all, and we cannot refuse to interest ourselves in those who will come after us to enlarge the human family. The reality of human solidarity, which is a benefit for us, also imposes a duty.[4]

The opportunities for nurturing this prayerful reverence, wonder, and stewardship are numerous. Obviously, one is travel. On long trips, our family looks for places to stop for lunch each day where we can soak in deep breaths of beauty (a creek, lake, a state park . . .). Guide books and detailed maps are helpful. We look for scenic routes whenever possible, bypassing interstates at times. Sunrise and sunset are often breath-taking moments, and can be included in one's driving time. Partially because of Kathy's and my love for nature, the children are beginning to notice things before we do on a trip. A willingness to stop the car on occasion, or at least to stop the conversation, and be silent and prayerful, as well as excited and sharing, about the beauty before us is important to us.

But most of the beauty we experience on a trip is also here at home. Routine and hectic paces keep us from seeing. There are flowers in our neighborhood no less beautiful to see and smell than in many a formal garden. But how often do we stop and smell them? Stars, rocks, creeks, leaves, shells, sunsets, sunrises, trees—everything except the ocean and the mountains is right here where we live. We are discovering that except for in winter, the time between work and dinner has often given a couple of us a chance to sit on the porch and notice things or spend a couple of minutes in the park at the end of our block. Native American parents have helped us come to see the importance of these moments in our children's development (and our own!).

We can even create a place of beauty right in our own home. Especially in February, when the redeeming qualities of winter—sledding, skating, etc.— have faded along with the brightness of snow, a little display of color or rocks or flowers can enliven one's senses and revive a drooping spirit. A friend of ours has suggested that everyone should be encouraged to create his or her own place of beauty in the home.

Cultivating our senses, along with our ability to experience things deeply, and learning how to express these experiences of God's creation and of God are part of this whole process of nurturing care and reverence. We are learning that expressing the meaning of a relationship, whether with another person, with nature, or with God, deepens that relationship and deepens ourselves. The more we express these relationships in words (prose or poetry), in music, in art, and so on, the more loving and reverent we become. Thus, encouraging our children to develop some way or ways of creative expression has a peace-and-justice dividend. Here, too, the joy we get from our own way(s) of creative (and prayerful) expression has a modelling effect on our children.

3. Integrating prayer and social action

Again, we want these two worlds—prayer and action—to come together in a single, faith-full life. We want the children to experience them together. An obvious way is to include the needs of others in our family prayers. The needs of relatives and friends are easy to include in family prayer (mealtime, bed-time, Mass). This circle can be expanded to include others—a person or group just described on a news program or in the paper, for instance, and especially people we are in touch with through our social action involvement.

The Shedd family has included in their family commitment a covenant in which each family member promises to pray daily for each other family member.[5] This is a way of concretizing prayer and deepening one's commitment to it, as well as a way of building family community. It is also one way of helping to direct children's prayers of petition toward people and away from things.

Prayer can be made explicitly a part of social action in other ways. Each time we passed the county jail while Gerald was in it, David would remind us to say a prayer for Gerald. Our Good Friday visit to the jail ended with a family prayer in the waiting room for Gerald and his mother. Many of the actions at General Dynamics include prayer. In seeking out people and groups involved in social action, one criterion to keep in mind is this integration of the spiritual and the political.

Concluding family meetings with a prayer for the grace of fidelity to the decisions and commitments of the meeting, especially if a service commitment was made, is another way to integrate the two worlds.

Family Adventures Toward Shalom suggests a more elaborate way of integrating prayer and social concern as the children get older.[6] It is called the "family litany." Here is a simplified version. Each family member receives a recent newspaper. (Parents or older children can work with the younger children.) Each person is to cut out an article or story that either distresses them or makes them hopeful. Then each person shares his or her story, and the family prays for the people involved. The prayer can actually be in the form of a litany, with the reader formulating the petitions and the rest of the family responding with something like "Lord, hear our prayer," or with a more spontaneous prayer.

4. Integrating social action and the liturgical year

There is a further opportunity for integrating the spiritual and the social/political in the social dimensions of the life of Christ as celebrated in the church year. The liturgical seasons can be used to educate for peace and justice. Both the seasons and the sacraments, especially the Eucharist (see 5, below), reflect the first of the "Mission Affirmations" of the Lutheran Church, Missouri Synod, which proclaim that "the church's ministries of worship, service, fellowship, and nurture all have a missionary dimension."[7]

The seasons of the liturgical year provide an excellent opportunity for integrating spirituality and social action. The spiritual message of each season contains a clear justice or social dimension. The year could be broken into two-month segments, with one home or parish liturgy in the course of each of these six segments that would integrate social concern.

a. December–January (Advent–Christmas): This is an ideal time to focus on simplicity and service. The symbol of the manger is clear and is very much a part of the life of most Christian families. Not as a king robed in splendor did he come. No, he came poor and homeless. Clearly Jesus came to serve and not to be served.

Our family Advent tradition revolves around this symbol of simplicity and service. Several evenings each week we gather at the manger, which we have built. The children take turns lighting the candles, one for each week of Advent. We reflect on the day that has passed and on some way in which we each have been able to serve others that day. As each of us shares this service experience, he or she places a piece of straw in our crib to make a softer place for Jesus to lie. This is how we prepare for his coming. Prayer and a song conclude the short ceremony. The symbol and ritual have become an important part of our family's growing tradition.

Pat and Ed and their six children also celebrate Advent in a service-oriented way. For Advent 1979 they paired with another family, and each regularly surprised the other with special prayers, notes, a visit, simple home-made gifts, and a morning together chopping down their Christmas trees. It made Advent 1979 a time of joyful sharing for both families.

Family Adventures Toward Shalom offers an interesting process for deciding upon and doing service during Advent.[8] Readings from Isaiah (2:1–4 and

11:4–11) on the meaning of *shalom* are the basis of a family discussion on the meaning of *shalom*. If there is time and interest, a "shalom box" can be made, in which the *shalom* actions (the service actions) suggested will be placed. The box is made by writing phrases or pasting pictures on the box that describe *shalom*. Then family members name various ways in which they can bring *shalom:*

—to the family (sharing jobs, fixing broken items, Kris Kringle surprises, spending time together, praying for one another)

—to the neighborhood (caroling, making gifts for neighbors, visiting someone we do not know and inviting them to go caroling)

—to the community/world (see Chapter 6).

A decision is made as to which suggestion(s) the family will carry out together. Finally, the Isaiah passages are re-read, followed by family prayer.

These same steps could be used throughout the year, with the Scripture readings adapted to the season.

b. February–March (Lent): The possibilities here are almost endless, since the connection with social action is so clear. As we write in the Preface of our Lenten program for elementary schools, *Responding to Jesus as He Suffers Today:*

Jesus suffered, died, and was raised from the dead for us. Although this happened 2,000 years ago, Jesus continues to suffer today. In our own country, as well as around the world, members of the Body of Christ suffer from neglect, greed, and oppression. Lent is an especially appropriate time for considering such persons and for responding to their needs, for numerous reasons. First, Lent is a time of repentance. Hunger, racism, and other forms of injustice are blatant expressions of human sinfulness. Secondly, Lent marks the institution of the Eucharist. The Eucharist is the celebration of our oneness as a human family in Christ. Neglect and oppression are a denial of this oneness, a denial of the Eucharist. Thirdly, Lent is the time for uniting with the passion of Jesus. His passion is being relived daily wherever people are neglected or oppressed.

Lent is a call to repentance or conversion. We are all called to turn away from selfishness and to follow Jesus as He goes up to Jerusalem to give His life for others. Thus, we are called to give our lives in service to others, especially to the suffering members of the Body of Christ. Our response to Jesus as He suffers today is two-fold: the works of mercy and the works of justice. First, as Veronica wiped the face of Jesus and Simon helped Jesus carry His cross, we too open our eyes to the needs of people around us and seek ways of helping them in their suffering. Secondly, we also look for ways of changing the situations, attitudes, and institutions that cause or contribute to this suffering in the first place.[9]

Concrete action possibilities for responding to Jesus as he suffers today are spelled out in the *Responding to Jesus* Lenten packet. Family action on world hunger during Lent is emphasized in our family Lenten program, *Those Who Hunger*.[10] A few of the action suggestions described in both these resources are presented in Chapter 6.

Fasting is a traditional part of Lent. One of the reasons people fast is to express their solidarity with others. Today, people fast to suffer and to identify, in a very small way, with the hungry of the world. Family efforts to simplify meals can free up money for both restocking a local food pantry and supporting hunger groups, like Bread for the World or Oxfam-America, working for social change. This year our own efforts at skipping occasional after-school/work snacks generated coins for the empty bowl on our dinner table, and ultimately for a local food pantry.

Another way to concretize our identification with Jesus in the suffering members of his body is to do walking, or outdoor, Stations of the Cross in our community. "Stations in the city" can be done by a single family, by several families, or by a larger church group. As we explain in the opening of Chapter 6, we suggest building action response as well as prayer response into one or more of the stations.

As with Advent, so too with Lent, symbol and ritual are important for the development of children's religious sense as well as the development of family tradition. The symbol we have come to use during Lent is the one we suggest in *Those Who Hunger*—a bowl of earth with a candle, which we place on our dinner table. This earth is a sign of repentance. On Ash Wednesday we receive a cross of dust or ashes on our foreheads as a sign that we are from the earth and will return to the earth (read Joel 2:12–19). The earth is also a sign of the ground into which the seed must fall if it is to bear fruit (read John 12:24–25). And the earth is a sign of food and the fruitfulness of God's creation, for the earth is the source of food; and so we pray as a family: "Lord, our God, you are the source of all goods, but we are your instruments. You save the lives of those in need, but you do it through us. During this Lent, help us to discover how to be a source of food for those who are hungry."

And we light the candle and pray, "Lord Jesus, we know that we will bear no fruit unless our branches, our lives, are rooted in you our vine. So we light this candle as a sign of your presence with us. We beg you, Lord, to walk with us in a special way during this Lent. May the flame of your love burn within us and express itself in courageous action."[11]

c. April–May (Easter): Our hope is rooted in the resurrection of Jesus. Jesus lives. Sin has been overcome. We are a saved people. We have already begun to live the Kingdom of God. Yet we know that the Kingdom of God is not yet fully realized. Hunger, racism, and other forms of injustice are very real and present in our world. It is the resurrection of Jesus that guarantees the ultimate fruitfulness of our present efforts to overcome injustice. If the seed falls into the ground and dies, it will bear fruit.

During this season, it might be appropriate to focus on social action that has a strong "Easter flavor." To us, "Easter flavor" means hope, and the action that inspires the most hope in us is being part of creating new ways of living and alternative institutions. Such efforts require deep hope, and are themselves a sign of hope for others: that things can be different, that we can create a different life for ourselves.[12] The action suggestions on stewardship, multiculturalizing family life, and creating non-sexist alternatives, offer many possibilities here. It might be helpful to put them into an Easter context and to see such efforts as part of our celebrating and living the Easter message.

A symbol of Easter life and hope could be built on the Lenten symbol of the bowl of earth. During Lent, seeds could be planted in that earth, so that they would blossom during Easter time.

d. June–July (Pentecost–Corpus Christi): Jesus sent his Spirit to transform his disciples and ultimately the world. Though few in number, the disciples touched many and the Gospel spread. That same Spirit works in us today. As the 1971 Synod of Catholic Bishops put it:

> The power of the Spirit, who raised Christ from the dead, is continuously at work in the world. Through the generous sons and daughters of the Church likewise, the People of God is present in the midst of the poor and of those who suffer oppression and persecution; it lives in its own flesh and its own heart the Passion of Christ and bears witness to His resurrection.[13]

The transformation of the world—accomplished through the Spirit's working in each of us—is what action for justice is ultimately about, and is an essential part of the Christian life. To return to that often quoted passage in *Justice in the World:* "Action on behalf of justice and participation in the transformation of the world fully appear to us as a constitutive dimension of the preaching of the Gospel." To celebrate Pentecost, then, is to allow the Spirit to work through us, through our action for justice. It is to allow ourselves to be sent forth into the world as a family.

Corpus Christi is the celebration of the Eucharist. The special relationship between the Eucharist and action for justice is described in the final part of this chapter.

e. August–September (New Beginnings): The beginning of school and the beginning of Fall provide a special opportunity for families to renew their commitment to service and social change. Summer will have brought some renewal of body and spirit. At this time of year there is often a readiness which the Spirit brings and uses to lead us to taking a next step in helping to build God's Kingdom. To celebrate this readiness with other families and to ask for insight and courage to take the next step would seem an especially appropriate theme for a liturgy at this time.

f. October–November (All Saints): The opening example of this chapter relates social action to this key day in the liturgical year. We are all called to be saints. Saints are people who gave themselves completely to the service of God and God's people, the Body of Christ. We focus on their lives, are inspired by their witness, and pray for the grace to imitate their generous response to the call of Jesus to serve.

5. The Eucharist and social action

We strongly agree with the 1971 Synod of Catholic Bishops:

The liturgy . . . can greatly serve education for justice. For it is a thanksgiving to the Father in Christ, which through its communitarian form places before our eyes the bonds of our brotherhood and sisterhood and again and again reminds us of the Church's mission [*Justice in the World,* Part III].

What this passage means to our own family is more concretely expressed in a prayer in *Those Who Hunger:*

Lord, in celebrating your Supper, we recognize and build your Body. We place on the paten at the Offertory ourselves and the whole human family in its constructive activities—our sisters and brothers rebuilding their lives and rebuilding cities; striving to make relationships work and make institutions work for people; struggling to overcome hunger and feed their families; people learning, sharing, caring for people and for the environment. Unite all these efforts and lives, Jesus, to your own. Transform them, as we lift them up to God as our act of unity, praise and thanksgiving.

In the chalice, Lord, to be united to your blood, we place all the blood spilled this day around the world—in prisons, in broken homes and lives, in areas of poverty and oppression, on battlefields, wherever racism and sexism and repression stunt peoples' lives. United to your blood, our own suffering and that of others will be redemptive and not be spilled in vain. This, too, Lord, we unite to your total gift on the cross and lift up to God.

Then, in receiving you back from God in Communion, Lord, we take into ourselves you as you are today—your whole body. When we say yes to you in Communion, we are saying yes to the whole human family united to you. We commit ourselves to deepening this realization of the oneness of the human family in our own hearts and to working for a fuller realization of this oneness in the world. Help us this day to discover what this means concretely for each of us, so that we can go forth from your Eucharist to, in the words of the Mass, "Love and serve the Lord."[14]

Difficult as church time often is for us, we have found a few ways of translating this prayer/vision for our children. Our commentaries whispered during the service or made on our way to church are our most regular opportunity. We mentioned above how at the Offertory we help the children name some gift(s) each of us can give to Jesus to give to God, and how at Communion we encourage them to talk with Jesus within them. Asking the children before the service or at the Prayers of the Faithful to pray with us for some suffering member(s) of the Body of Christ is another step. Recently we have begun to work with them after Communion on identifying some member of the Body of Christ to whom we can say a fuller yes that day or week.

Some time in the future we plan to focus on the penitential aspects of the liturgy. We want the children to begin to understand "social sin"—sin that is embedded in institutions and societal attitudes and practices. It is for these sins as well as for our own personal sins and shortcomings that we can ask for forgiveness: "Lord have mercy" on us for our corporate greed and national wastefulness as well as for our own desire for comfort and convenience. "Lamb of God, you take away the sins of the world"—closing hospitals and schools in poor areas, building ever more destructive weapons while hunger increases, imprisoning and torturing people for their political or religious convictions, enticing the poor to buy luxuries for the sake of profit—"have mercy on us." Yes, Lord, *on us,* all of us, for we are one family.

For Gandhi, the real power of nonviolence—the power to bring about social change—came up out of an inner or spiritual force. It is this power that manifests itself in us when we become aware of and live the oneness of life. This interior oneness is both symbolized in, and built up by, the celebration of the Eucharist.

As Gandhi so well showed us, there are not two worlds, two lives—our "spiritual life" and our social action life. Doing justice is not the *application* of our religious faith. It is its very substance. For, as the prophet Jeremiah has told us, to do justice is to know God:[15]

Woe to him who builds his house by unrighteousness, and his upper rooms by injustice. Did not your father eat and drink and do justice and righteousness? Then it was well with him. He judged the cause of the poor and the needy; then it was well. *Is this not to know me?* says the Lord [Jer. 22:13,15–16; italics added].

CONCLUSION

SPRINGS, BOWS, AND ANCHORS

The decision to rear children has profound consequences. It is not a part-time job, nor is it something you do for a few years before moving on to other responsibilities. It demands enormous time and energy and sacrifice, and so parents find themselves having to say no to many of life's "extras." Social action or social justice often appears to be one of those "extras" that we just have to say no to.

This book has tried to show that our commitment to parenting can be precisely one of the basic ways in which we can live out the Gospel call to justice and peace. Rather than experiencing frustration at how little time is "left over" for social concerns, we discover that parenting abounds in ways to integrate social concerns into family life.

We have to remember that it is the quality, not the quantity, of the actions or learning experiences we provide for ourselves and children that is most important. Perhaps more than anything else, it is the quality of our love and presence—patient, faithful, joyful, forgiving—that matters most. It is quite possible to become so concerned with the external or social mission of our families that we jeopardize the quality of our presence within the family.

Three images were presented in this book that suggest the quality of parental love we mean. These images summarize the ways in which we bring together the external and internal missions of the family. As parents, we are to be "springs whose waters never run dry" (Isaiah), "bows" whose arrows are our children (Gibran), and "anchors of love in a sea of violence" (Boulding).

As springs of water, we must be life-giving, nurturing, bubbling at times, refreshing, preparing our children to go forth. We must feed spirit as well as body.

As bows from whom God sends forth our children into the world, we are to inspire and to guide. We must instill desire, initiative, and courage, then let the arrows fly.

Finally, as anchors, we must provide the acceptance and security without which our children will not be able to fly. Our fidelity—that we keep caring for each other, for them, and for others—can provide much of the stability our children need to go forth in confidence.

But we parents also need to be watered—to have both our imaginations stretched and our wounds healed. We too need to be inspired and sent forth. And we too need anchors of support and love. This book has shown that there are obstacles to taking up the social mission we are called to as families. But we hope this book has been a spring of possibilities, too, breaking open the imagination. And we hope that our reports of the struggles of families to remain faithful through failures as well as successes have inspired all of us to renew our efforts to go forth with greater creativity and courage. Finally, this book has underlined the urgency of supportive community—the importance of going forth together in order to overcome our isolation and fear.

Springs, bows, and anchors—for one another, for other families, and especially for our own children. We water them, let them fly, and harbor them at their return, each day, in a repeating cycle down the weeks and months, a spiral over the years, a journey together into the world and its loving Creator.

If you do away with the yoke, the clenched fist, the wicked word, if you give your bread to the hungry, and relief to the oppressed, . . . Yahweh will always guide you, giving you relief in desert places. He will give strength to your bones and you shall be like a watered garden, like a spring of water whose waters never run dry [Isa. 58:9–11].

APPENDIX

How the Church Can Encourage Families in Their Social Mission

(In preparation for the 1980 World Synod of Catholic Bishops on the "Role of the Family in the Contemporary World," the Family Life Department of the U.S. Catholic Conference asked a number of experts to present papers on the synodal theme at a special preparatory meeting of the American Bishops at the University of Notre Dame, June 15-18, 1980. The authors were asked to present the "Social Mission of the Christian Family"; following is an adaptation of a portion of their testimony. The complete text [50 pages] is available from the Institute for Peace and Justice, St. Louis, MO 63103.)

Despite the spread of community in the Church, many families still feel isolated. In their isolation, they feel powerless and overwhelmed—overwhelmed by the complexities of problems around them, overwhelmed often by the struggle to survive, and even overwhelmed by the Church's social teaching. Much needs to be done, and can be done, to assist families in facing the social dimension of Christian life. This assistance is necessary at all levels of Church, from the parish up. Following are some suggestions for assisting families in their social mission, at the parish, diocesan, and national levels.

A. At the Parish Level

1. *Direct involvement in social issues*

Besides educational programs and preaching that address social issues, there are many ways in which the parish's concrete action can encourage, legitimize, and model responsible involvement in social issues. In terms of the five social issues described in this paper, here are several possibilities for parish action.

a. On Stewardship
—Parishes can help organize recycling campaigns.
—Parishes can promote simplicity in their social and fund-raising events.
—Parishes can encourage stewardship by making parish facilities available to others. Openness of rectory and convent calls families to a similar openness with regard to their homes.

b. On Racism
—Parishes can promote minority participation in leadership roles in parish committees, in worship, and in other parish functions.

127

—Parishes can multiculturalize liturgical and educational materials. As the 1979 U.S. Catholic Bishops Pastoral Letter on Racism, *Brothers and Sisters to Us,* puts it, "The Church must respect and foster the spiritual . . . gifts of the various races and peoples and encourage the incorporation of these gifts into the liturgy" (p. 13).

—Parishes can support the desegregation of local schools and refuse to allow the parish school to become a haven for families fleeing integration.

—Parishes can, again in the words of the Pastoral Letter on Racism, "avoid the services of agencies and industries which refuse to take affirmative action to achieve equal opportunity and . . . itself always be a model as an equal opportunity employer" (p. 13).

c. On Sexism

—Parishes can promote the participation of women in leadership roles in parish committees, in worship, and in other parish functions. As *Justice in the World* affirmed, "Women should have their own share of responsibility and participation in the community life of society and likewise of the Church" (Part III).

—Parishes can show sensitivity in the use of language in the liturgy and other public parish activities and avoid sexist language whenever possible.

d. On Militarism/Violence

—Parishes can promote global awareness through pairing with other churches/ missions in other parts of the world.

—Parishes can observe the annual World Day of Peace, and, in the United States, make sure that the peace dimension of the Respect Life Program is included in parish programming.

—Parishes can see to it that the Church's teaching on war and military service is disseminated, and that, when appropriate, adequate counselling is available to youths facing military service.

2. Raising Social Consciousness

Woven throughout our seven chapters above are three components, or strategies, for our ongoing formation in social awareness and social action. All of us need to experience the call to social action as a call from Jesus, as an integral part of our faith. We need to be touched by the victims of injustice and by those who are giving their lives for those victims. Finally, we need to experience social action in the context of community, where we will be supported, challenged, held accountable, and broadened in our vision and in the possibilities for action. The parish can do much in terms of each of these components.

a. Experiencing the social mission as a call from Jesus

—As we mentioned above, the liturgical year offers numerous opportunities to see the social dimension of the life of Jesus. While the entire Gospel, and thus the readings for all seasons of the liturgical year, have a social dimension, it can be made explicit in various ways at certain special times like Advent, Christmas, Lent, Easter, and Pentecost.

—The celebration of the Eucharist is central to the nurturing of social commitment. Besides what was mentioned in Chapter 7, pastors and parish liturgy committees might consider ways of incorporating Christian service and social action into the liturgy. For instance, in some parishes the Christian service commitments of those being confirmed (and of their parents) are presented at the Offertory of a Sunday parish liturgy. In other parishes the Eucharistic ministers carrying Communion to the sick are sent forth from the Sunday Mass *with their families* by the worshipping community.

—Communal celebrations of the Sacrament of Reconciliation can and should include reflection on social sin as well as personal sin, as noted in *Justice in the World* (Part III).

—Parishes can and should include adult education programs that integrate social action and spirituality, such as the *Those Who Hunger* program mentioned in Chapter 7.

b. Being touched by advocates for justice and victims of injustice

—Parish adult education opportunities as well as religious education for youth can and should include programs that bring parents and children into contact with people who can inspire them and help them see how to work for justice as families. Christian service needs to become an integral part of the curriculum in all Christian schools.

—Pairing suburban and inner-city parishes where real reciprocity or exchanges occur is an excellent means of encouraging concrete social action.

—A parish resource center with books, audio-visuals, and magazines that put parishioners in touch with the victims of injustice as well as the statistics of injustice, is another excellent means.

c. Being supported in community

—The recommendations from the "Call to Action" program, the Catholic Bishops' Bicentennial program in the United States, included a section on "Family." This document calls for "pastoral programs which encourage formation of family groups for prayer, worship, sacramental preparation, marriage enrichment, family life education and mutual support, either within parishes or across parish boundaries."[1] Such prayer, worship and parenting education groups can and should work toward the integration of spiritual life and apostolic life, family ministry and social ministry.

—The formation of a parish social action or Christian service committee not only legitimizes such activity as integral to Christian living, but also creates the possibility for joint action, along with all the support, challenge and accountability that a group can provide.

—A parish skills bank and other mechanisms whereby parishioners can pool and share their resources encourage simplicity, stewardship, and community. A parish vegetable garden can likewise encourage these values, while putting people in touch with the earth.

B. At the Diocesan and National Level

With some overlapping, the suggestions that follow fall into three main categories, which might be termed structural integration, education, and public encouragement.

1. Structural Integration

The integration of family ministry and social ministry does not happen just by wishing it to or calling it to happen. The social mission of families must be integrated into diocesan and national programs and structures. Several possibilities exist.

—Parents who are integrating social ministry into their family life need to be part of family life organizations, programming, and resources, in order to bring about the Call to Action recommendation that

> organizations and movements which specialize in marriage and family life include and/or develop programs dealing with the social justice dimension of family life and provide materials, models, resources and skills to enable families to open themselves to the injustices in the world, to reach out to those in need, and to provide channels through which they can contribute to the solution of such problems of injustice ["Family," II, 2].[2]

—As a dimension of this recommendation, a diocesan resource center for getting family social action resources into parishes and homes seems essential.

—All diocesan and national committees, commissions, and councils that relate to family life, need members, especially family members, who have integrated social justice into their ministry.

—Parish social action or justice and peace committees need to be supported and resourced by similar diocesan and national committees.

—Religious education efforts to integrate education for peace and justice into Christian schools and parish schools of religion need to be supported and resourced at the diocesan and national levels. Educators with competence in education for peace and justice need to be part of diocesan school and religious education offices as well as similar national offices.[3]

2. Education

—In-service educational opportunities in education for peace and justice for school administrators and teachers need to continue at both the national and diocesan levels, so that schools can encourage the family's social mission.[4]

—Efforts to integrate social justice into seminary programs should be expanded and encouraged at both the diocesan and national levels.[5] Especially important is helping priests understand and model the integration of social justice and spirituality, so that this vision can be more widely communicated in the Church.

—Similarly, homily aids and clergy education programs integrating social justice and spirituality, and examining ways of assisting families to integrate family ministry and social ministry, are needed.

—"Educational programs for effective parenthood," as the Call to Action recommendations put it, and marriage/family enrichment programs like the Christian Family Movement, Marriage Encounter, and family and married couples' retreat programs, need to be developed or expanded and made more accessible to families.

—Diocesan, regional, and national pastoral letters on crucial social issues educate Christians on these issues and on their role in working for justice and peace, as well as encouraging individual Christians, families, and institutions to fulfill their roles.

3. Public Encouragement

—The willingness of the institutional Church to address social problems, particularly their own part in these problems, makes a significant difference for families and others with regard to their own commitment. Where dioceses and national con-

ferences of bishops have taken courageous stands on affirmative action, school desegregation, Church investments, the arms race, workers' rights, and the like, then
families feel supported as well as led in their own participation in the Church's social
mission. Conversely, dioceses and national conferences which refuse to address these
issues place a very real obstacle in the way of families carrying out their social mission.

—Diocesan media channels can and should play a prominent role in publicly encouraging families to carry out their social mission. Features in diocesan newspapers
on families responding to the Church's social mission, as well as regular reporting of
social issues and the Church's responses to these issues, inform, inspire, and increase
imagination. The television and radio apostolate is a similar source for public education and encouragement.

—There are other, less formal, ways in which dioceses can encourage families to
integrate social action into their lives. A climate of open dialogue, where advocates of
change have access to diocesan decision-makers, is a climate which encourages action
for justice. A letter or call of support from the Bishop can often make a great difference. Public recognition of individuals and families working for justice and peace
not only encourages the individuals involved, but also legitimizes this whole dimension of living the Gospel.

RESOURCES

Chapter 1

Alternative Celebrations Catalogue. Alternatives, P.O. Box 1707, Forest Park, GA 30050, 1978, $5.00. This book contains many concrete suggestions about how to celebrate at traditional times (Christmas, Hannukah, weddings, birthdays, etc.) in ways that are simple. It also is filled with suggestions about buying gifts from self-help groups in the Third World. It is an invaluable resource for families of every description.

Alternatives: An Alternate Lifestyle Newsletter. Same publisher, $5.00 a year. This newsletter is a continuous aid and reminder about ways to make voluntary simplicity a way of life.

Easterday, Kate Cusick. *The Peaceable Kitchen Cookbook: Recipes for Personal and Global Well-Being.* New York: Paulist Press, 1980. This book is a wealth of recipes and helpful suggestions about vegetarian cooking. Its theme is that of peaceful relationships with people around the world.

Gibson, William E. *A Covenant Group for Lifestyle Assessment.* New York: United Presbyterian Program Agency, 1978. This book will be helpful as a guide for a study and/or action group dealing with the issues of simplicity and stewardship. It includes scriptural and prayerful reflection as well as practical suggestions for action.

Longacre, Doris Janzen. *Living More with Less.* Scottdale, Pa.: Herald Press, 1980. Both beautiful and practical. Part I examines the basic principles (do justice, learn from the world community, nurture people, cherish the natural order, and nonconform freely) that underlie the specific suggestions for lifestyle change in Part II. Using the witness and stories of dozens of families, Longacre offers a lifetime of possibilities for simplifying money, clothes, homes and homekeeping, transportation, celebrations, recreation, and meals, and for strengthening one another. As Ronald Sider puts it in his Introduction, this is "an excellent combination of theory and practice."

Stewardship Papers. Pax Christi USA, 3000 N. Mango Ave., Chicago, IL 60634. $.50 per Paper. This series of papers deals with different aspects of stewardship. The first one, "The Family and Stewardship," by Mary Ellen and Charles K. Wilber, is particularly appropriate to the topic of this chapter. The Wilbers give concrete examples from their family of nine about how they have attempted to build an atmosphere of stewardship.

Strangers and Guests: Toward Community in the Heartland. A regional Catholic Bishops' Statement on land issues, May 1, 1980. Heartland Project, 220 S. Prairie

Ave., Sioux Falls, SD 57104. The principles of land stewardship that are set forth in this statement are a good source for prayer and reflection, as well as for discussion in families.

Television Awareness Training. New York: Media Action Research Center, 1976. While this manual is geared specifically for television awareness training, its articles as well as its worksheets will be helpful to families and will be interesting for older children in some of their groups.

Chapter 2

Bows and Arrows: A Newsletter for Family Enrichment (published quarterly by Interpersonal Communication Services, 7052 West Lane, Eden, NY 14057) is a delightful eight-page newsletter on all aspects of promoting nonviolence in and through the home. The articles are short and practical, include reviews of books for children and parents, and sometimes relate nonviolence and family social action possibilities to the church year.

Dreikurs, Rudolf. *Family Council: The Dreikurs Technique for Putting an End to War Between Parents and Children (and Between Children and Children).* Chicago: Henry Regnery Co., 1974. An elaborate and effective description of family meetings, how to start them, and the moral basis for this dimension of family life. It includes examples from specific families to make the theory more concrete.

Gaulke, Earl H. *You Can Have a Family Where Everybody Wins: Christian Perspectives on Parent Effectiveness Training.* Saint Louis: Concordia Publishing House, 1975. As the subtitle indicates, Gaulke takes the basic principles of "parent effectiveness training," shows how they parallel many of the principles of the New Testament, and provides some practical examples. A good book if you want a Christian version of Thomas Gordon's *Parent Effeciveness Training* (New York: Peter H. Wyden, Inc. 1970).

Haessly, Jacqueline. *Peacemaking: Family Activities for Justice and Peace.* New York: Paulist Press, 1980. As the mother of five children (preschool through adolescence), committed to justice and peace in both the home and the world, the author has many practical suggestions on nonviolence in the home, especially on creating an affirming and cooperative environment.

Judson, Stephanie. *A Manual on Nonviolence and Children.* Philadelphia: Friends Peace Committee, 1977. A wealth of games, techniques, observations, and insights on developing nonviolence in children, especially pre-school and elementary ages. Though not a parent, the author writes effectively for parents as well as for teachers.

Lechner, Bettye. *Empowering Families: A Manual of Experiences for Family Sharing.* Saint Paul, Minn.: National Marriage Encounter, 1977. This 65-page booklet contains a series of family meeting topics, with directions for carrying out the sessions. It is a good resource for supplementing family meeting agendas that focus solely on business items or problem-solving.

Prutzman, Priscilla, et al. *The Friendly Classroom for a Small Planet: A Handbook on Creative Approaches to Living and Problem Solving for Children.* The Children's Creative Response to Conflict Program (P.O. Box 271, Nyack, NY 10960, published by Avery Publishing Group, Wayne, New Jersey, 1978). Excellent for affirmation exercises, practice activities for teaching creative problem-solving, and conflict resolution ideas. For parents and teachers of preschool and elementary school children.

Shedd, Charlie. *Promises to Peter: Building a Bridge from Parent to Child.* Waco, Texas: Word Books, 1970. A practical, humorous account of family living in the Shedd household. Challenging ideas on problem solving, discipline, and independence in children. Especially helpful for parents with teenagers.

Chapter 3

McGinnis, James and Kathleen, et al. *Educating for Peace and Justice.* Saint Louis: Institute for Peace and Justice, 1981. This four-volume set is geared specifically for teachers, but it contains many ideas that will be helpful to parents. See especially the units in Volume II on *War* and *Global Interdependence.*

Tolley, Howard. *Children and War: Political Socialization to International Conflict.* New York: Teachers College Press, 1973. This book is good background reading for adults on how children's attitudes toward war are formed. There are definite implications for parents in terms of the necessity of dealing with the issue in the home.

See also Aldridge, Robert and Janet. *Nonviolence and the Family Community.* Cited under Chapter 6.

See also Haessly, J. *Peacemaking: Family Activities for Justice and Peace.* Cited under Chapter 2.

See also *Try This: Family Adventures Toward Shalom.* Especially the sections on "Creative Conflict," "Caring for and Sharing the World's Resources," and "Valuing All People." Cited under Chapter 6.

For further materials:

Global Education Associates, 552 Park Ave., East Orange, NJ 07017, a non-profit educational organization which does consultant work, conducts workshops, and develops materials on various world order topics; and Women's International League for Peace and Freedom, 1213 Race St., Philadelphia, PA 19103, a national organization with offices in many cities, particularly for its materials on early childhood education.

Chapter 4

Council on Interracial Books for Children *Bulletin* Volume 11 (1980), nos. 3 & 4, "Children, Race & Racism: How Race Awareness Develops." This special issue deals with ways to help children develop positive attitudes about themselves and others, how to help children deal with racist name-calling, how race awareness develops. It is a thought-provoking resource for parents of all racial groups. A subscription to the *Bulletin* is $10/year for individuals and $15/year for institutions.

Goodman, Mary Ellen. *Race Awareness in Young Children*. New York: Collier Books, 1964. $1.50. This is a cultural anthropologist's study of how racial attitudes begin to form in four-year-olds. It still ranks as one of the most important research studies in the area and is excellent background reading for parents.

Kohl, Herbert. *Growing with Your Children*. Boston: Little, Brown and Company, 1978. A parenting book that deals well with the issue of white children and racism. Kohl's basic premise is that "children first learn racism consciously or unconsciously from their parents." He gives specific suggestions about how to create healthy racial attitudes.

McGinnis, Kathleen. *Cultural Pluralism in Early Childhood Education*. This booklet was prepared for the Early Childhood Education office of the Lutheran Church, Missouri Synod. It contains ideas for educators as well as parents on ways to evaluate what is done with young children in terms of the development of racial attitudes. It also contains a recommended book list for young children. Available through the Institute for Peace and Justice, 2913 Locust, Saint Louis, MO 63103, $2.50.

McGinnis, James and Kathleen, et al. *Educating for Peace and Justice*. Saint Louis: Institute for Peace and Justice, 1981. See Volume I, units on *Multicultural Education* and *Racism*. Cited under Chapter 3.

Latimer, Bettye I., ed. *Starting Out Right: Choosing Books About Black People for Young Children*. Wisconsin Department of Public Instruction, 1972, $2.50. This booklet lists criteria helpful in selecting books about Black people for young children. It also contains a book list that will be helpful for parents.

For further materials:

The Council on Interracial Books for Children, 1841 Broadway, New York, NY 10023, produces a variety of materials. Here are two filmstrips-with-cassettes of special note in the area of multiculturalizing family life:

"Unlearning 'Indian' Stereotypes" will help students learn new facts about Native Americans—past and present—while they "unlearn" common stereotypes about "Indians."

"Identifying Racism in Children's Books" demonstrates both blatant and subtle ways in which racist messages are transmitted to children through books.

Chapter 5

Carmichael, Carrie. *Non-Sexist Childraising*. Boston: Beacon Press, 1977, $9.95. This book has more relevance for parents of younger children, although all could benefit from the thought-provoking issues raised, ranging from participatory childbirth to sexism in schools.

Guidelines for Selecting Bias-Free Textbooks and Storybooks. Council on Interracial Books for Children, 1841 Broadway, New York, NY 10023, $6.95. This book is an excellent tool to use to evaluate reading material for children in terms of the images presented of different races, of men and women, of older people, and of disabled people.

Hart, Carole; Pogebin, Letty Cottin; Rodgers, Mary; and Thomas, Marlo, editors. *Free to Be You and Me.* New York: McGraw-Hill Book Co., 1974, $6.95. This compilation of stories, poetry, songs, dialogues, essays is a delightful way to introduce the more serious realities of how sexism limits the development of young men and young women. It is especially valuable for young children, but will be enjoyed by all ages.

"Identifying Sexism in Children's Books." Filmstrip-with-cassette produced by the Council on Interracial Books for Children, New York. This audio-visual highlights the ways sex-based stereotypes are perpetuated through children's books and is especially useful for triggering parent-child discussion. Available through the Council on Interracial Books for Children, 1841 Broadway, New York, NY 10023. (Their catalog is free and describes other materials as well.)

Chapter 6

Aldridge, Robert and Janet, *Nonviolence and the Family Community,* as yet an unpublished manuscript (631 Kiely Blvd., Santa Clara, CA 95051), is an engaging account of the authors' family's venture into nonviolence—in their home, with ten children, and in their resistance to militarism in the United States. An especially moving and encouraging book for parents with children in their teens and twenties.

Lersch, Phil and Jean, *Hunger Activities for Children* (121 pages) and *Hunger Activities for Teens* (15 pages), both published by Brethren House, 6301 56th Avenue North, Saint Petersburg, FL 33709, contain a great variety of group activities, some of which are adaptable for family use, around the issue of hunger. They are integrated with Scripture and involve action possibilities as well as learning activities.

McGinnis, James. *Those Who Hunger.* New York: Paulist Press, 1979. A Lenten hunger program that integrates prayer, Scripture, and traditional Lenten practices with action possibilities for changing our lifestyles as well as addressing some of the economic causes of hunger. Family activities are included in each section. Appropriate for individual family use as well as for groups.

Ecumenical Task Force on Christian Education for World Peace. *Try This: Family Adventures Toward Shalom.* Discipleship Resources, P.O. Box 840, Nashville, TN 37202, 1979. Most helpful on the themes of social action, prayer, and stewardship, but useful throughout. Especially valuable for use in a group setting (as a family education program); but many activities are also appropriate for individual families. Geared to parents of both elementary and secondary-school-age children.

See also *Peacemaking: Family Activities for Justice and Peace,* Chapter 2, for an additional resource of social action possibilities for families.

Your Family Called to Action is the guide book for family social action published by the Christian Family Movement (P.O. Box 792, Whiting, IN 46394) for use in the 1980s. The "Social Inquiry" process of CFM has parent groups *observe* the facts of a social issue, *judge* it in relationship to Christian principles, and *act* on the issue. The process is integrated with prayer and Scripture. This "Inquiry Book" (63 pages) examines a range of issues, including racism, sexism, world peace, the elderly, the disabled, simplicity of lifestyle, and political responsibility. Good suggestions for action and a very supportive process for parent groups.

Chapter 7

Seitz, Susan. *Becoming Fully Alive: Home Activities Handbook*. Office of Religious Education, 1229 Mt. Loretta Ave., Dubuque, IA 52001. A religious education manual for family play, reflection, and home worship. Geared to parents of preschool and elementary-school-age children.

Westcott, Patricia, et al. *Home: Resources for Family Sharing*. New York: Paulist Press, 1978. Sponsored by the Catholic Office of Religious Education in Dubuque. This book contains a wealth of family activities centered around the liturgical year and integrating creativity, reflection, and prayer. It also includes activities around U.S. holidays and material for evaluating TV commercials. Geared to families with children of all ages, but probably more appropriate with elementary-school-age children.

See also *Those Who Hunger* (cited under Chapter 6) and *Promises to Peter* (cited under Chapter 2) for additional resources that integrate family prayer with family activities.

NOTES

INTRODUCTION

1. "Declaration on Christian Education," 3, in *The Documents of Vatican II* (New York: Guild Press, 1966), p. 641.

2. Vicki Breitbart with Barbara Schram, "The Politics of Parenting Books: How to Rock the Cradle Without Rocking the Boat," *Bulletin* of the Council on Interracial Books for Children, vol. 9 (1978), nos. 4 and 5, p. 3 (see "Resources," above.)

Chapter 1

1. "Letter of Chief Seattle," as quoted in James McGinnis, *Bread and Justice* (New York: Paulist Press, 1979), pp. 322–23.

2. *Report* of the 1978 Mission Consultation, 118th General Assembly of the Presbyterian Church in the United States, quoted in *Constituency Education Pilot Program,* Church World Service, 1979, p. 90.

3. Gustavo Gutiérrez, *A Theology of Liberation* (Maryknoll, N.Y.: Orbis, 1973), pp. 300–301.

4. Palo Alto Packet Committee and Simple Living Program, *Taking Charge: A Process Packet for Simple Living: Personal and Social Change* (American Friends Service Committee of San Francisco, 1975), p. 2.

5. Ibid., p. 70.

6. Ibid., p. 73.

7. Ibid., p. 13.

8. Frances Moore Lappé, as quoted in Ecumenical Task Force on Christian Education for World Peace, *Try This: Family Adventures Toward Shalom* (Nashville: Discipleship Resources, 1979), p. 8.

9. Palo Alto, *Taking Charge,* pp. 44–45.

10. *Try This: Family Adventures Toward Shalom,* p. 43.

11. In T. C. McLuhan, *Touch the Earth* (New York: Outerbridge & Dienstfrey, 1971), p. 6.

12. *Television Awareness Training* (New York: Media Action Research Center, 1976), p. 67.

13. James McGinnis, *Those Who Hunger* (New York: Paulist, 1979), p. 15.

Chapter 2

1. Rudolf Dreikurs, *Family Council: The Dreikurs Technique for Putting an End to War Between Parents and Children (And Between Children and Children)* (Chicago: Regnery, 1974), pp. 4, 5, 8.

2. Robert and Janet Aldridge, "Nonviolence and the Family Community" (as yet unpublished manuscript, 631 Kiely Blvd., Santa Clara, CA 95051, 1980), ch. 7, p. 3.

3. Dreikurs, *Family Council,* p. 17; see also pp. 15–20.

4. Thomas Gordon, *Parent Effectiveness Training* (New York: Wyden, 1970), chapters 9 and 10.

5. Sadie E. Dreikurs, "Foreword," in Dreikurs, *Family Council.*

6. Ecumenical Task Force on Christian Education for World Peace, *Try This: Family Adventures Toward Shalom* (Nashville: Discipleship Resources, 1979), p. 58.

7. Charlie Shedd, *Promises to Peter (Building a Bridge from Parent to Child)* (Waco, Texas: Word, 1970), pp. 12–15.

8. Adapted from Priscilla Prutzman et al., *The Friendly Classroom for a Small Planet (A Handbook on Creative Approaches to Living and Problem Solving for Children)* (Nyack, N.Y.: Children's Creative Response to Conflict Program, 1978), p. 8.

9. Elise Boulding, *The Personhood of Children* (Philadelphia: Religious Education Committee, Friends General Conference, 1975), p. 13.

10. Cf. Gordon, *Parent Effectiveness,* pp. 139–47.

11. Dreikurs, *Family Council,* p. 7.

12. Ibid., p. 27.

13. Shedd, *Promises,* pp. 38–39.

14. "Effects of Spanking," *Bows and Arrows,* vol. 3, no. 4 (Winter 1980), p. 4.

15. Kahlil Gibran, *The Prophet* (New York: Knopf, 1965), pp. 18–19.

Chapter 3

1. Quoted in *Peace on Earth* (8th Day Center for Justice, 22 E. Van Buren, Chicago, IL 60605), section, "Ordinary Time."

2. Religious Society of Friends, *Faith and Practice* (Philadelphia: Friends, 1972), p. 35.

3. "The Church in the Modern World," Pastoral Constitution of the Second Vatican Council, 1965; quoted in *Peace on Earth,* section, "Eastertide."

4. Voice of America broadcast, 1951, as quoted in *Peace on Earth,* section, "Eastertide."

5. *1980 Resource Catalog,* Institute for Peace and Justice, 2913 Locust, Saint Louis, MO 63103.

6. Quoted in T. C. McLuhan, *Touch the Earth* (New York: Outerbridge & Dienstfrey, 1971), p. 120.

7. Howard Tolley, *Children and War: Political Socialization to International Conflict* (New York: Teachers College Press, 1973), p. 58.

8. Ibid., p. 112.

9. Norma R. Law, "Children and War," a position paper for the Association for Childhood Education International, 3615 Wisconsin Ave., N.W., Washington, DC 20016, February 1973, p. 233.

10. *Television Awareness Training* (New York: Media Action Research Center, 1976), p. 26.

11. Ibid., p. 24.

12. "Bishop Pulls Kids out of Sub Fest," *Sojourners,* April 1980, p. 6.

13. Quoted in *The Associates Newsletter,* January–February 1980, p. 6 (Global Education Associates, 552 Park Ave., East Orange, NJ 07017).

14. Tolley, *Children and War,* p. 36.

15. Daniel J. Berrigan, S.J., "The Arms Race and the Hole in the Ground," *New Catholic World,* May–June 1979, p. 110.

16. Ecumenical Task Force on Christian Education for World Peace, *Try This: Family Adventures Toward Shalom* (Nashville: Discipleship Resources, 1979), p. 32.

17. Tolley, *Children and War,* p. 124.

18. Women's International League for Peace and Freedom, 1213 Race St., Philadelphia, PA 19103.

19. Ecumenical Task Force, *Try This,* p. 15.

20. Robert and Janet Aldridge, "Nonviolence and the Family Community" (manuscript, 631 Kiely Blvd., Santa Clara, CA 95051, 1980), ch. 11, p. 9.

21. For more information on the Nestlé boycott, contact: INFACT, 1701 University Ave., S.E., Minneapolis, MN 55414.

22. David King, *International Education for Spaceship Earth,* New Dimensions Series, No. 4 (New York: Foreign Policy Association, 1970), p. 73.

23. Quoted in *Peace on Earth,* section, "Christmastide."

Chapter 4

1. U.S. Catholic Bishops, *Brothers and Sisters to Us: Pastoral Letter on Racism in Our Day* (Washington, D.C.: U.S. Catholic Conference, 1979), pp. 6–7.

2. Religious Society of Friends, *Faith and Practice* (Philadelphia: Friends, 1972), p. 33.

3. *Bulletin* of the Council on Interracial Books for Children, vol. 9 (1978), nos. 4–5, p. 11.

4. Abraham Citron, *The "Rightness" of "Whiteness": The World of the White Child in a Segregated Society* (Detroit: College of Education, Wayne State University, 1969), p. 14.

5. Adapted from Council on Interracial Books for Children, *Stereotypes, Distortions and Omissions in U.S. History Textbooks* (New York, Racism and Sexism Resource Center for Educators), p. 131.

6. "Unlearning 'Indian' Stereotypes," filmstrip of the Council on Interracial Books for Children, 1978. From the reading script.

7. Some of these guidelines are adapted from Council on Interracial Books for Children, *Guidelines for Selecting Bias-Free Textbooks and Storybooks* (New York: Racism and Sexism Center for Educators, 1980), pp. 24–26.

8. *Racism in America and How to Combat It* (Washington, D.C.: U.S. Commission on Civil Rights, 1970), Clearinghouse Publication, Urban Series No. 1 (January 1970), p. 5.

9. Council on Interracial Books for Children, *Definitions of Racism,* March 1974.

10. Ibid.

11. Ibid.

12. Letter from Leroy Zimmerman to Chairperson of Boy Scout Circus, St. Louis, Mo., Nov. 1978.

Chapter 5

1. Council on Interracial Books for Children, *Stereotypes, Distortions, and Omissions in U.S. History Textbooks* (New York: Racism and Sexism Resource Center for Educators, 1977) p. 131.

2. Council on Interracial Books for Children, *Human and Anti-Human Values in Children's Books* (New York: Racism and Sexism Resource Center for Educators, 1976), p. 11.

3. *Justice in the World,* Chapter 3, "Practice of Justice," in David O'Brien, ed., *Renewing the Earth: Catholic Documents on Peace, Justice, and Liberation* (Garden City, N.Y.: Image, 1977), p. 400.

4. Personal correspondence from Marilyn M. Breitling, Coordinator, Coordinating Center for Women in Church and Society, United Church of Christ, July 1980.

5. Carrie Carmichael, *Non-Sexist Childraising* (Boston: Beacon, 1977), p. 5.

6. *Checklist on Sexism,* from Council on Interracial Books for Children (see Resources, above, for the Council's address).

7. See *Fact Sheet on Institutional Sexism,* Council on Interracial Books for Children, January 1979.

8. Somewhat adapted from "Ten Quick Ways to Analyze Children's Books for Sexism and Racism" in *Guidelines for Selecting Bias-Free Textbooks and Storybooks* (New York: Council on Interracial Books for Children, 1980), pp. 24–26.

9. Carmichael, *Non-Sexist Childraising,* p. 2.

10. Elaine Laron, "The Sun and the Moon," in Ms. Foundation, Inc., *Free to Be You and Me* (New York: McGraw-Hill, 1974), p. 136.

Chapter 6

1. Charlie Shedd, *Promises to Peter* (Waco, Texas: Word, 1970), pp. 37–38.

2. Phil and Jean Lersch, *Hunger Activities for Children* (Saint Petersburg, Florida: Brethren House, 1978), is a source of numerous activities by which children learn about hunger by doing. See Resources, above.

3. From James McGinnis, "A Hope Garden and More," in *Those Who Hunger* (New York: Paulist Press, 1979), p. 6.

4. *Alternative Celebrations Catalogue* (Ellenwood, Georgia: Alternatives, 1978), 4th Ed., pp. 113–114.

5. James McGinnis, *Those Who Hunger,* Section 2.

6. Jacqueline Haessly, *Peacemaking: Family Activities for Justice and Peace* (New York: Paulist, 1980), pp. 70–71.

Chapter 7

1. Elise Boulding, "Practicing Quakerism at Home," *My Part in the Quaker Adventure* (Philadelphia: Religious Education Committee, Friends General Conference, 1964), Revised Edition, pp. 129–134.

2. Susan Seitz, *Becoming Fully Alive (Home Activities Handbook)* (Dubuque, Iowa: Office of Religious Education, 1976), p. 33.

3. "Letter of Chief Seattle," *Fellowship,* December 1976.

4. Pope Paul VI, *On the Development of Peoples,* 17.

5. Charlie Shedd, *Promises to Peter* (Waco, Texas: Word, 1970), pp. 76–77.

6. Ecumenical Task Force on Christian Education for World Peace, *Try This: Family Adventures Toward Shalom* (Nashville: Discipleship Resources, 1979), p. 12.

7. "The Mission Affirmations" adopted at the Forty-Sixth Convention of the Lutheran Church, Missouri Synod, Section I.

8. Ecumenical Task Force, *Try This,* p. 5.

9. James McGinnis, *Responding to Jesus as He Suffers Today (A Lenten Program for Elementary Schools)* (Saint Louis: Institute for Peace and Justice, 1979), "Introduction."

10. James McGinnis, *Those Who Hunger* (New York: Paulist, 1979).

11. Ibid., "Prayer Service," 1.

12. Ibid., 7.

13. *Justice in the World* (Washington, D.C.: U.S. Catholic Conference, 1971), "Conclusion."

14. McGinnis, *Those Who Hunger,* p. 6.

15. Cf. John C. Haughey, ed., *The Faith That Does Justice* (New York: Paulist, 1977), p. 76.

Appendix

1. Among other places, these recommendations appear in a tabloid entitled *A.D.1977,* published by the Quixote Center, P.O. Box 651, Hyattsville, MD 20782; section on "Family," I, 3, c (page 10).

2. Ibid., II, 2 (page 10).

3. *To Do the Work of Justice* (Washington, D.C.: United States Catholic Conference, 1978), p. 7:

We ask all Catholic educational institutions, including elementary and secondary schools, to insure that their students are exposed to fundamental Catholic social teaching as reflected in papal encyclicals and pronouncements, conciliary and synodal documents and episcopal teaching. At the same time, we strongly urge dioceses to seek actively to extend career opportunities in the areas of social ministry and justice education.

We request each diocese to initiate an in-service justice education program for teachers, school administrators and school boards, as well as health care personnel. We request that diocesan offices of religious education develop programs of preparation for the sacraments which will highlight their social as well as individual dimension. Finally, in dioceses where such instrumentalities do not exist, we recommend that consideration be given to the establishment of agencies to promote and coordinate justice education and social action; or, where this is not possible, that the sharing of resources and programs on a regional basis be investigated instead. In this connection, we pledge the assistance and support of the USCC Department of Social Development and World Peace.

4. Ibid.

5. Ibid., pp. 5–6:

To those responsible for directing seminaries, we encourage in-service courses, workshops and seminars for faculties and administrators to help them develop programs of justice education and we request that these programs be strengthened. Seminarians and others preparing for ministry should continue to be instructed in the social thought of the Church and have a variety of experiences with social problems and cultural conditions in order to deepen their awareness of injustice and develop the knowledge and skills which will enable them to provide leadership in the Church's mission of justice and peace.

We request that preparation for ministry for justice continue to be included as an integral part of pastoral preparation in seminaries. Commitment to the promotion of justice should continue to be among the criteria used in evaluating candidates for ordination. We ask the NCCB Committee on Priestly Formation to assess carefully the commitment to justice ministry on the part of a seminary within the committee's regular program of seminary visitation.

Other PARENTING FOR PEACE AND JUSTICE Resources
by Kathleen and James McGinnis

Parenting for Peace and Justice (1980), a series of five 60-minute cassette tapes recorded live. Each 30-minute presentation is followed by questions that ask the McGinnises to apply their principles and examples to single-parent families, families with teenagers, families with very young children. The tapes parallel Chapters 1, 2, 4, 5, 6, and 7 combined. The set, including an attractive vinyl album cover, is $25.00 plus $2.00 mailing.

Christian Parenting for Peace and Justice: Families in Search of Shalom (1981) is the Program Book published by the Board of Discipleship of the United Methodist Church. It offers parish family life or adult education leaders, marriage encounter leaders, and others six formats for leading adults or whole families through "parenting for peace and justice." Formats include adult and intergenerational weekends, a series of weekly sessions, small discussion groups, couple and family dialogues. Each of the seven units/sessions, corresponding basically to the seven chapters in the book, offers a variety of activities (from Scriptural reflection and prayer to action possibilities on the theme) with detailed directions to the program leader. Approximately 85 pages; tentatively $4.95, plus $1.00 mailing.

Families in Search of Shalom (1981), is a 100-frame, 10-minute filmstrip that accompanies the Program Book and presents the bibilical vision underlying "parenting for peace and justice" and introduces each of the themes in this book. The music, visuals, and text are upbeat, affirming, and inviting to families as well as challenging. The filmstrip serves as an excellent introduction to the whole area of "parenting for peace and justice" and can be used to interest people in the other resources or a program. $25.00, plus $2.00 postage.

National Parenting for Peace and Justice Network (NPPJN) is an ecumenical effort initiated by the McGinnises and a national advisory board to help families deepen their own commitment to integrating family life and social ministry and encourage other families to do the same. A quarterly newsletter provides practical suggestions for action, new resources for families, information about parenting for peace and justice workshops and training opportunities for program leaders, and a variety of other items. Individual membership is $10.00 a year; organizational memberships are also available. Write the McGinnises for futher information.

The Social Mission of the Christian Family (1980) is the full statement of the McGinnises to the U.S. and Canadian Bishop Delegates to the World Synod of Catholic Bishops on "The Role of the Family in the Contemporary World." This fifty-page paper is a more theoretical statement of how materialism, racism, sexism, and militarism affect families, especially in the Western World, and how families can address themselves to these issues and become agents of change in their society. $2.00, plus 50 cents mailing.

All these resources are available from the McGinnises at the Institute for Peace and Justice, 2913 Locust, St. Louis, MO 63103; 314-533-4445. Make checks payable to the Institute and please enclose payment with your order.

NATIONAL PARENTING FOR PEACE AND JUSTICE NETWORK
(NPPJN)

This network was formed as a national ecumenical effort of parents interested in deepening their own commitment to blending family life and social ministry and helping other families do the same. We want to reach out to families and to religious and secular organizations serving families—through a variety of resources, workshops, and programs. Program leaders are being identified and training opportunities are being developed. Local and regional coordinators are volunteering in various parts of the country to provide an outreach and to encourage others to work with them in making these presentations.

Individual, organizational, and denominational memberships provide the funding for the NPPJN. Individual membership is $10.00 per year and provides a copy of the Network Newsletter and other NPPJN mailings. For further information, membership, or resources, contact:

Jim & Kathy McGinnis
NPPJN
Institute for Peace and Justice
2913 Locust
St. Louis, MO 63103
(314) 533-4445

Beginning May 1, 1982
NPPJN will be located at
Institute for Peace and Justice
4144 Lindell Blvd.
St. Louis, MO 63108
(314) 533-4445